DON'T GET SCAMMED
SCAMMED

GET SMART!

2/12/20

DON'T GET SCAMMED
GET SMART!

Seven Simple Steps
to Becoming a Savvy Consumer

*To Caroly,
Stay safe!*

CONSUMER INVESTIGATOR DALE CARDWELL

WITH JUDY KIRKWOOD

*Dale
Cardwell*

BOOKLOGIX®
Alpharetta, GA

ISBN: 978-1-63183-650-3 - Paperback
eISBN: 978-1-63183-651-0 - ePub
eISBN: 978-1-63183-652-7 - mobi

Library of Congress Control Number: 2019911578

Printed in the United States of America   0 8 1 3 1 9

♾This paper meets the requirements of ANSI/NISO Z39.48-1992 (Permanence of Paper)

For my mother, Carolyn Cardwell,
who told me I could,
and my father, Bill Cardwell,
who showed me how.

CONTENTS

PREFACE ix

— PART 1 —

INTRODUCTION
WHY SHOULD I TRUST DALE CARDWELL? 3

CHAPTER 1
THE ELEMENTS OF A SCAM 11
 The Rip-Off Range 14
 The Three Emotional Elements of a Scam 21

— PART 2 —

CHAPTER 2
FAST FUNDS FOUND (FFF) 29
 Fast 32
 Funds 34
 Found 36

CHAPTER 3
DEFINE YOUR DEAL 41
 Define Your Product 47
 Define Your Offer 49
 Define Your Price 52

CHAPTER 4
ENSURE YOUR DEAL   57
Ensure Ethical Negotiation   60
Ensure an Equitable Contract   63
Ensure an Effective Guarantee   71

CHAPTER 5
AUTHENTICATE YOUR DEAL   77
Authenticate References   80
Authenticate Reviews   85
Authenticate Reports   88

CHAPTER 6
LEGITIMIZE YOUR DEAL   93
Legitimize by Checking Licensing   99
Legitimize by Checking Liability Insurance   101
Legitimize by Doing a Lawsuit/Background Check   104

── PART 3 ──

CHAPTER 7
I'VE BEEN SCAMMED! NOW WHAT?   109
What You Should Know about the Court System   114
Get Your Documents in Order   116
Determine Intention   117
Harness the Power of Online Reviews   120
Make a Stink   122
File a Criminal Complaint   124
Seek a Criminal Warrant without Police Aid   124
File a Civil Complaint   125
File an Official Report   126

CHAPTER 8
TrustDALE AND BUILDING A COMMUNITY OF TRUST   129
The Role of the Consumer   131
The Role of the Company   133
Where TrustDALE Fits In   135

APPENDIX
COMMON SCAMS, CONS, AND SCHEMES   141

ACKNOWLEDGMENTS   153

PREFACE

This is a simple book. In fact, think of it as a handbook to becoming a smarter consumer.

As a longtime investigative reporter, I noticed common denominators when it came to consumers who got burned by a scam. Each situation was a combination of consumer ignorance (or greed) and a variation of traditional deceptive, double-dealing, shimmy-shammy, flim-flam cons and hustles that really haven't changed much over the years. Just about every night on the six o'clock news, I would showcase an example of someone who had lost money, or worse, due to a lack of preparation before making a deal and misplaced trust in an individual or company. The consequences ranged from frustrating and time-consuming to catastrophic.

If I could chase down and expose the "bad" guy who tricked the consumer into thinking he or she was getting a bargain, I would try to get restitution for the "victim." My purpose was to protect the viewing audience from making the same mistakes as the hapless consumer by learning from these cautionary tales of con artists in our local communities and nationwide. This has been the pattern of TV consumer journalism since its inception: show and tell a sad story of an ordinary person being taken advantage of by a bully, feel sorry for the victim, try to bust the perpetrator, and teach from example.

One day, while watching a "bait-and-switch" commercial on TV, I realized there was a better way. You see, in advertising every-one claims to be the best. They tell you, "We arrive on time!" "Our people are background-checked!" "We have the best warranties in the business!" The fact is that most information mediums (internet, TV, radio, print) will allow advertisers to claim anything they want, whether it's true or not. The result? *Caveat emptor*—buyer beware.

I realized I could make a difference by educating consumers pro-actively, instead of retroactively, teaching them what scammers know that consumers don't. This was my opportunity to level the marketplace playing field.

Part 1 of *Don't Get Scammed: Get Smart!* begins with a pivotal moment in my life that crystalized my mission to tell the truth. Next, I share observations based on thirty years of experience that show you how to recognize a scam, what defines the Rip-Off Range, and how scammers trick consumers into trusting them. The stories I include throughout this guide reinforce how to iden-tify the elements of a scam.

Part 2 presents my seven steps to becoming a savvy consumer. You can think of it like playing a game—offense and defense. The first three steps are the components of a term I call **Fast Funds Found (FFF)**, or the defense, which applies to three tricks of the scam trade to keep in mind when someone approaches you with an unexpected offer. All you have to do is ask yourself 1) if you are being offered a deal that relies on making a fast decision, 2) if your deal relies on a sudden windfall of funds, and 3) if your salesperson/business owner can be found in the future.

The next four steps require strategic offense, or proactive participation and practice, but guarantee you will not be easily scammed. I came up with an easy-to-remember acronym for this process, **DEAL**, where each letter relates to a step **(Define, Ensure, Authenticate, and Legitimize)** to safeguard yourself and the people you love against being ripped off.

Be warned: the bad guys are aware of how consumers can protect themselves too, and will try to figure out ways around these safeguards. My DEAL steps are pretty tight, however, because they're based on years of investigative experience. Plus, they have worked for me in my own business.

Every chapter begins with a story of a person I've encountered in my career who has made one or more common errors in agreeing to a deal that was not in their best interests. These striking tales of abuse of the public's trust will motivate you to never be roasted like a sitting duck.

If you absorb the simple concepts of FFF, practice the four steps of DEAL, and recognize the red flags of a scam, I am confident you will make the right decisions. But remember, every deal or agreement you enter into is a new challenge, so keep this handbook handy.

Someone's getting scammed right now, so let's get going!

INTRODUCTION

WHY SHOULD I TRUST DALE CARDWELL?

Thirty minutes after Sheriff-Elect Derwin Brown was murdered, half a dozen police officers were at my door, informing me that they had reason to believe I was going to be killed. I was shepherded into protective custody along with my family.

—Dale Cardwell
December 15, 2000
DeKalb County, Georgia

I honed my investigative skills for consumer protection as a television journalist. My specialty was pulling back the curtain on the Wizard of Oz and exposing exactly what people in power do not want the rest of us to see. Sheriffs, mayors, governors, politicians, and top administrators do not take kindly to that kind of reveal. But my passion was uncovering corrupt behavior and standing up for the rest of us who live by a code of ethics.

3

December 15, 2000, was a pivotal moment in my life. I had to decide whether to be safe, by withdrawing from high-profile criminal investigations, or sorry, because that would mean giving up my calling as someone the public could trust to tell them the truth. There were certainly times I could have ended up dead, of use to no one. But this death threat was real, and involved my family.

In 2000 I did a series of reports about a sheriff in Georgia's DeKalb County as part of the news team for the ABC affiliate in Atlanta. Hope was in the air in 1996 when career deputy Sidney Dorsey became the first African American to be elected sheriff in DeKalb County. But after only a few years, it became known that he was significantly corrupt, though no one could prove it. This was nothing new, since every sheriff in the suburban Atlanta department since 1964 had been investigated, indicted, or imprisoned. But it was regrettable.

Someone I did not know gave me information that indicated Sheriff Dorsey was using his on-duty deputies to provide manpower to his own private security firm. They would clock in at the sheriff's department, then go to a bank, for instance, in another county, and pass the time they would normally be on duty for DeKalb County as a security guard at the bank. This was convenient since Dorsey didn't have to pay them anything for working at the bank or worry about things like paying into workers' comp.

I began documenting the situation with photographs so I could report what was happening. My investigation was uncovering more and more dirty tricks and harmful actions that could not be ignored.

Partly due to my reporting, Dorsey's competitor for the sheriff's position in 2000, Derwin Brown, won in a forced runoff. Dorsey's camp was filled with such sycophants and toadies that never in his worst dream could he have imagined losing the razor-close election. It was a stunning victory for the highly qualified, and so far uncorrupted, Derwin Brown.

Brown began cleaning up the sheriff's department before he was officially sworn in. Besides the double-duty scandal under Dorsey, his councilwoman wife had bussed prison inmates into the Dorseys' neighborhood to paint houses and do yardwork for the sheriff's primary supporters, and there were sexual-harassment charges against Dorsey and his department. Brown had already served thirty-eight people in Dorsey's inner circle with notices they were going to be terminated when he took office. Those people—who all had considerable scams going, as evidenced by their six-figure incomes when their annual salaries were just over $30,000—were not happy.

What happened next was unbelievable. Sheriff-Elect Derwin Brown was murdered in his driveway at about midnight, three days before his swearing in. He had been at a party celebrating his victory with family and friends and was walking to his door with roses for his wife's birthday when he was shot twelve times.

This is when the police showed up at my door. We were under police protection for several weeks in different hotels, but I continued to report developments in the story for the TV station, taking different routes and using decoy cars. After it was deemed safe for my family to return home, the TV station hired a former secret service agent to teach us how to protect ourselves and be safer in our everyday lives.

It was presumed that the murder of Derwin Brown was a hit ordered by Sidney Dorsey, but it was such a rainy night that there was virtually no physical evidence for arrests—and no one was talking. The police could not find the weapon, and Dorsey and his inner circle had alibis.

Sidney Dorsey was not arrested and sentenced to life in prison until 2002. His former deputy, Patrick Cuffy, who had orchestrated the attack on Dorsey's behalf, was given full immunity in return for testifying against Dorsey and others involved. He moved back to the Caribbean islands, where he was from, and remains a free man.

You may think this has nothing to do with consumer education to safeguard citizens from marketing scams, false advertising, and con men and women. But that wild ride had a profound impact on me. What I learned was that I will not be intimidated by any business or individual who counts on the public's ignorance.

Eventually I left conventional TV reporting to start TrustDALE, not because I lost my love for reporting, but because I was driven to make a bigger impact. I wanted to not only stop bad guys in their tracks, but create a community of trust, where consumers could get great products and services at fair prices and companies could sell those products and services at a fair profit. My character and skills led me to verify the truth, expose lies, and put together consumer offers with superior service in a way that would benefit both seller and buyer, with neither making out like a bandit and both contributing to a win/win.

Practices like these are basically stealing from people—not just money, but trust.

I have never lost my sense of wonder at how scammers, including reputable companies, can operate in the Rip-Off Range, devising one scheme after another to make consumers feel as if they are being treated special rather than being taken advantage of.

Practices like these are basically stealing from people—not just money, but trust.

Corrupt political scenarios did not sit well with me, and neither do age-old scams that, while packaged differently for contemporary consumers, serve the same purpose: to fool the public into thinking they are getting a deal when they are really getting shot in the foot.

Let's take a dive into the most common scams consumers need to be informed about. Some of the stories in this book will shock you, but they are all true. My goal is for you to identify the red flags before signing a contract or agreement, or sending or wiring money anywhere, and avoid getting scammed.

THE JOURNEY TO TrustDALE

The first time I felt the sting of being treated unfairly was in 1969 in Hueytown, Alabama. I was flat on my back with my arms and legs pinned to the ground. My brother, Bruce, two and a half years my senior and forty pounds heavier, was the offending party. It wasn't enough for Bruce to have me completely at his mercy. Bruce's special brand of brotherly torture was to drool and dangle a bead of saliva over my face as I twisted helplessly from side to side trying to avoid the inevitable. Moments after my humiliation, I burst into my house, ran to my mother who was drinking coffee with a friend, and started blubbering out what had happened. Seconds into my story, she stopped me—as she always did—and said, "If you don't get out of this house right now, I'll spank both of you!"

Nearly fifty years later, I consider that experience (and all the times it was repeated) to be among the most valuable lessons of my life. I am grateful to have been and to be a little brother, and by the way, I love my brother Bruce with all my heart. Today he is my right-hand man, president of our family's publishing division, and next to my wife, Angie, my closest confidant. But constantly being the underdog, and having my experience devalued, instilled in me a deep desire to seek justice, expose people who intentionally harm others, and when possible, help the victims recover what was lost, including dignity.

By the time I was out in the world working, I understood not everyone was on the same page as me. There were many who not only "got away with murder," they walked away with a bonus check, chuckling at the naiveté of the general population.

My first real taste of professional success came on the heels of the worst military aviation tragedy in US history. I was a green reporter just two months into my first newsroom job at WKAG in Hopkinsville, Kentucky. The station was independent, meaning it had no network affiliation, in a town so small it wasn't listed as a television market important enough to be measured for viewer ratings. Its only distinction is that Hopkinsville is the bedroom community of Fort Campbell, Kentucky, a sprawling 102,000-acre military post on the Kentucky-Tennessee line. Fort Campbell is the home of the 101st Airborne Division: twenty-nine thousand soldiers who train to drop out of the sky from helicopters into hostile territories—usually as first responders in war zones. The Screaming Eagles, as they are known, made their name in World War II, dropping into Normandy, France, as part of Operation Overlord.

December 12, 1985, was one of the division's darkest days. A DC-8 carrying 248 Fort Campbell soldiers and 8 crewmembers crashed shortly after takeoff from an airstrip in Gander, Newfoundland. The soldiers were returning home after six months of peacekeeping duty in Egypt. All onboard were killed. As the cub reporter at my station, I mostly had mop-up duty, covering "page-two" aspects of the story while our more seasoned reporters interviewed family members and officials. My career and life changed significantly four days later, when I took a call in the newsroom early on Sunday morning.

"I'm calling because my sister was engaged to one of the soldiers who died on that plane," the young woman said. "This might not be important, but they communicated by exchanging cassette tapes because phone calls were so expensive. His last cassette tape arrived Wednesday, the day before the crash. On it, he said he and the men on the flight were scared to fly on that plane because it was in such bad shape."

As soon as I heard those words, the hair stood up on the back of my neck. I instinctively knew this would become a major international story. But first, I had to win the confidence of a seventeen-year-old woman who'd just lost her fiancé. Second, I had to acquire the cassette tape, shoot the interview, and figure out the logistics of getting that story to the networks in New York.

I figured it out. Monday, December 16, my report featuring the story of Tracy Walker, her late fiancé Army Specialist Jeffrey Scott Key, and his fellow soldiers' fears of flying on the army-charted jet was the lead story of the CBS Evening News. It was also carried by ABC, NBC, CNN, and every major paper in the country. More importantly, the story prompted Congress to temporarily suspend the use of non-military-owned chartered aircraft like the Arrow Air DC-8 that crashed in Gander until a thorough investigation was conducted into the cause of the crash and whether non-military charters should be used at all. In the words of then Kentucky Congressman Carroll Hubbard, "We as members of Congress can see to it that they didn't die in vain because we can urge and insist and demand that the Federal Aviation Administration and the Department of Defense in the future see to it that our American troops are transported on planes that are just as safe as Air Force One." In the end, it was determined the plane crashed due to heavy ice on its wings.

It was extremely satisfying, as well as humbling, to know I played a small but important role in an investigation that changed United States military policy. It was also intoxicating. That feeling followed me throughout my television news career and was repeated every time I busted a bad guy and prevented him from harming others. But there was something missing.

The "missing" thing for me with my exciting investigative news career was personal purpose. It wasn't enough for me that I was warning future would-be victims. There had to be more that I could do, and I knew I had more to offer. One night while leading the newscast and, as I like to say, telling people how rotten the world was, I had an epiphany. I realized, in one moment, that I had spent twenty-five years of my life learning what people did wrong that played into the hands of con artists and scammers, which inevitably resulted in not only financial loss, but a loss of trust. I had a vast storehouse of knowledge, that was for sure. In this seminal moment, I realized I could "flip the coin" and shift my knowledge and talent from being reactive to proactive. I could protect people IN ADVANCE of making a difficult buying decision. I had found my life's purpose.

CHAPTER 1

THE ELEMENTS OF A SCAM

DALE'S CASE STUDY FILES
Monumental Fraud: Delia

Shortly after burying her husband of fifty-two years, Delia received a condolence call from Daniel Lemon. She didn't know Lemon, but he said he was a close friend of her son's and knew he was taking the death of his father hard. Lemon mentioned he happened to be in the monument business. Since he did his marketing online and via mail, rather than having a physical place of business, he had very little overhead and could pass on the savings to his customers.

The stone for her husband, Jeffrey, had already been selected, but Delia felt she would like to honor her brother with a monument to be installed before Veterans Day. She chose one from the glossy brochure Lemon sent her and mailed him a check for $353. The monument never showed up, and after a few months Lemon stopped making excuses for the delay and quit returning her calls.

Delia, who was in a vulnerable state to begin with considering her recent loss, was heartbroken. She called the TV station where I worked as a consumer reporter to ask for help.

My heart sank when I realized Lemon had no address, just a post office box. Obviously he did not want to be found. However, it turned out he was using his real name for his monument business, as I found when I checked magistrate court records, where I discovered several judgments against Lemon for failure to deliver a product after payment. I also tracked down his home address through the court records. Unfortunately, he had not made good on repaying any of the money associated with the judgments awarded to his victims.

The morning after the night we ran the story of "monument scammer" Daniel Lemon, I had twenty-three voicemails from other consumers who had been robbed of their money for monuments for their loved ones. Pooling information, I learned Lemon was an assistant manager at a large local grocery store. His sideline, or "hobby," was taking advantage of grieving spouses listed in obituaries and spinning the same tale he told Delia about being friends with one of the children of the deceased.

I went to his home with a camera crew and caught him coming home after a work shift. He was shocked when I said, "I just want to know how you sleep at night," on Delia's behalf—for which he had no answer.

Within a few weeks, seventeen additional cases had been filed against Lemon in magistrate court. This was a clear case of intent to defraud. Is there anything more heinous than taking advantage of the elderly who are grieving the loss of a life partner?

The district attorney saw things differently. Prosecutors called the transactions "business disputes," not thefts, and would not pursue criminal charges. Lemon did lose his job with the grocery store chain as a result of public backlash against his morbid con game. But his victims were out both money and monuments, and something even more important: trust in humanity. Delia was grateful for the TV station's help. But Lemon's victims, who were trying to do something kind for those they'd loved and lost, could not even count on the court system to support their quest for justice. They were left feeling helpless all over again.

What I want you to learn from this handbook is how to protect yourself from people like Daniel Lemon, who don't care who they rip off as long as they get away with it. And they *can* get away with it—partly because they know how to run a scam, and partly because our court system, police enforcement, and sheriff's departments are imperfect avenues of recourse for victims of fraud.

This country loses billions to scams every year. MSNBC reports that seniors alone lose an estimated $2.9 billion annually due to financial exploitation, according to the Senate Special Committee on Aging. (Impersonating the IRS was the number-one scam targeting seniors in 2018.)

> *Similar to viruses that evolve through changes in their DNA and mutate into strains that survive by adapting to their host environment, scams have mutated with technology.*

It would be impossible to identify every scam that's been perpetrated on consumers. I believe it's far more beneficial to help you recognize the core elements of scams rather than put a name on them, like the Nigerian Prince scam or the Ponzi scheme. Similar to viruses that evolve through changes in their DNA and mutate into strains that survive by adapting to their host environment, scams have mutated with technology. The delivery method changes (mail, telephone, internet), but the core is consistent.

THE RIP-OFF RANGE

"Rip-Off Range" is a term I use to address issues that pertain to people who are defrauded of $500 to $50,000. The limit varies depending on your income, but if you have lost less than $500, you may not go to the police. If it is more than that, most people will try to get their money back. Good luck, and here's why. You're going to quickly learn that law enforcement and the court system are not going to help you. I know this may seem shocking—after all, you've been ripped off! But the "system" doesn't see it that way. One reason is caseload. Most police departments, sheriff's offices, and prosecutors are focused on violent crime, so they are quick to categorize your loss as a business dispute to be solved in civil court. Another factor pertains to motive, as in your motive. Grizzled police and court veterans know many victims are enticed into fraud by believing they can get something for nothing. In other words, for better or worse, they believe you made your own bed.

"Rip-Off Range" is a term I use to address issues that pertain to people who are defrauded of $500 to $50,000.

Here's the exception, and the reason I set the upper limit of the Rip-Off Range to $50,000. It's been my experience that people who lose this amount often have the financial resources to manipulate the system into coming to their aid. They "know" people (attorneys, judges, local officials) and can afford to spend even more money to punish those who took advantage of them.

Getting caught in the Rip-Off Range is what I call realizing the world does not have a daddy. When people in the Rip-Off Range begin investigating their deals gone bad, they are stunned to find out there is no "consumer police force." Con artists know this. Courts and government know this. Law enforcement departments know this. Media knows this because they report on scams and see the shock on victims' faces when they realize no government authority will take action on their behalf.

Who doesn't know this? Consumers who have not yet been scammed, which means they are ripe for picking, packing, and being sent to the cleaners, to mix metaphors.

In addition, the laws of each state are full of escape opportunities for perpetrators of fraud: they don't show up for court dates, and nothing happens other than the granting of a continuance and another court date; they can continue committing fraud while they are involved in a court case; when the consumer finally gives up because it costs too much time and money to fight, there is no penalty for the defendant. Even if the consumer wins a case, there may be no money to collect; or the defendant may appeal the verdict to a higher court and start the cycle all over again.

The bad guys know that if you wire or send them money in a different state, there will be disputes over jurisdiction that will take time to settle; that if they take their tarnished reputation to a different county, no one will know about it because law enforcement agencies do not interact with each other. What's really sad is to see the consumer intentionally get the runaround from the people sworn to protect them. I'll get into that in the upcoming case study.

To avoid getting scammed by a con artist, you have to be smarter than the individual who has targeted you. You have to know what they know. Their patterns are clear, and they have discovered they can do whatever they want and not be held accountable. Scammers know all the ways to evade legal and law enforcement entities. Here are two stories from the Rip-Off Range.

The first involves a screened porch that a man standing behind Kathy in the Home Depot checkout line offered to build after he overheard her express her desire for one. Walter, the contractor, started it but never finished it. His excuses included getting a heart stint and being upset after hitting a boy on a bike. Even though Walter only showed up for work once, Kathy continued to pay him because she understood life can interfere with work sometimes. Then she noticed every check she sent him had been cashed at a different bank. After paying Walter $8,200, the only thing Kathy had to show for it was a mess in her backyard. Meanwhile, Walter had stopped answering Kathy's phone calls, and was unreachable since he was not at the address he had given her.

At that point, Kathy tried to file a criminal complaint in her home county of Forsyth. The county first told her she needed to file her complaint in Walter's home county of Cherokee. When Kathy attempted to file in Cherokee County, she was told she had to file where the offense took place—Forsyth County. Every time she filed, by the way, it cost her $100 to $200.

After being ping-ponged between the two counties, she was finally allowed to file a civil complaint in Forsyth County Magistrate Court. But since the Forsyth sheriff's department doesn't serve summonses outside Forsyth County, Walter could not be served. Next, Kathy attempted to hire a private service company to serve Davis, but the Forsyth County magistrate judge wouldn't approve the private server she hired.

Frustrated at her inability to get help, Kathy contacted TrustDALE.

We first gave Walter a chance to explain himself. He wouldn't answer Kathy's phone calls, but was eager to meet with our producer, who posed as a potential client. When Walter showed up to estimate the cost of a porch, we asked him why he had taken Kathy's money and not built her porch. He said he had filed for bankruptcy, but would pay Kathy back. We knew that wasn't going to happen without some outside force holding his feet to the fire, so we got involved in trying to help Kathy get someone to hear her case.

We visited the Forsyth County Magistrate Court when Kathy again attempted to get a criminal warrant on her own. We were as puzzled as Kathy when the magistrate judge asked Kathy why what Walter had done constituted a crime.

"Because he took my money with no intention of performing the job," said Kathy.

"Why is that a crime?" asked the judge.

Perplexed, Kathy answered, "What do you want me to say?"

"I can't tell you what to say," the judge replied. "It's not my role to tell you what to say."

The judge was obviously playing a game to get Kathy to give up. For one thing, Kathy was not represented by an attorney, and even though it is not required, judges would rather deal with attorneys. In addition, although courts are public places throughout the US and videotaping is allowed, the judge was only okay with us videotaping anything but her, which seemed to us a case of vanity. It was definitely not a good fit for Kathy to get justice.

Finally, through the persistence of both Kathy and TrustDALE, including demonstrating similar contractor agreements Walter had bailed on, the Forsyth County sheriff charged Walter with theft. He was given the option of pleading guilty and receiving a ten-year probated sentence on the condition he pay Kathy back. If he failed to do so, he would go to prison. The whole process took over a year.

Over this period of time, Kathy felt violated by Walter and mocked and ignored by public officials. She was stunned to learn the law enforcement community didn't feel any responsibility to pursue Walter, and that the judge had actually debated whether taking money for doing nothing was a crime.

To help restore Kathy's faith that someone does care about what happens to consumers, TrustDALE paid for the removal of the debris Walter left in her yard, which was evidence of plain bad execution of the screened-porch project. It never would have held up, nor ever been worth $8,200.

The same thing happens over and over, where things seem stacked against the consumer seeking not only restitution, but to stop the scammer (thief) from doing the same thing to other people. Why should it be so hard for consumers to get a hearing and a judgment? For one thing, scammers know if they show up even once and begin the work, it constitutes some kind of effort on their part, even if they never finish. For another, the law is complicated and these cases tend to drag on and on, with missed attendance at hearings that just provide more clutter for courtroom dockets.

Car purchases and repairs are notorious for Rip-Off Range scams because there are so many opportunities for things to go wrong, costing a consumer more money than they thought. Pamela's experience, however, is not your garden-variety car story.

When Pamela dropped off her car at Big Guy's Auto to have work done, she never imagined her work vehicle would be out of commission for over a month. Every time she called to pick it up, she was told there was something else wrong with it that had to be repaired. But the time element is not what upset her.

After she finally picked up the car, she drove forty miles and the clutch burned out. But that was not the core issue either.

What Big Guy's Auto did not know was that Pamela had an electronic witness to what happened to her car while it was in their possession. As a Progressive insurance client, Pamela had enrolled in their Snapshot program that tracked her driving with a chip that was installed in her car. The chip stores information on how far the car is driven each day and how hard it is driven. It can tell Progressive, for instance, if the driver hits the brakes too hard, and it shows the driver's patterns so the insurance company can reward good drivers and penalize bad ones.

When Pamela checked the chip information online, she was shocked to see her car had been driven 1,042 miles while it was supposedly being repaired. Her clutch was burned out *and* the engine had been blown after driving the car only forty miles. To add insult to injury, she heard from Progressive that her rates were going to go up as a result of her poor driving skills. (She was able to prevent that from happening by explaining her situation.)

The issue was that while Pamela's car was supposed to be sitting safely at Big Guy's, some yahoo had commandeered it as his personal free-ride service, and not only driven it over a thousand miles, but driven it so recklessly that the engine and clutch were ruined. Pamela not only wanted the money she had paid for repairs, but compensation for taking the car elsewhere to address the burned-out clutch and blown engine. Pam couldn't believe it when the manager told her she was lying, that no one had mis-used her vehicle, and hung up on her. Pam's next call was to the local sheriff's department. She was allowed to file a report, but detectives told her it was a business dispute that needed to be settled in civil court.

Precisely because there is no consumer police in our society, TrustDALE often steps in as a proxy. Where else can wronged consumers turn to?

When Pamela didn't get any satisfaction from Big Guy's or law enforcement, she called TrustDALE. We first tried to settle the sit-uation over the phone. There are times well-intentioned people simply fail to communicate effectively and misunderstandings fly out of control. Our team can often settle those issues with a third-party conversation. Red flags appear, however, when the proprietor is never available, will not return our call, or is as rude to us as they were to their customer. Our call to Big Guy's went nowhere. Because Pamela reported to us that the woman who coordinates jobs at Big Guy's had told her an employee named Taco drove her car back and forth every day because he had to test it, we took our camera crew to ask her about Taco and his road tests. Any mechanic will tell you a car need not be driven more than twenty to forty miles to test-drive its roadworthiness after repairs. On camera, she denied saying any such thing, plus she insisted that the car had been at Big Guy's for only three days and that someone else must be responsible.

We didn't buy that for one minute, but when law enforcement was contacted they told Pamela her issue with Big Guy's Auto was a business dispute and not a criminal case with grounds for arrest. She would have to go to court to pursue any solutions.

Knowing what a time-consuming, expensive process prosecution would be, we contacted one of our certified partners, AAMCO, to ask if they could check out the car and fix any problems so Pamela could at least drive it. They ended up doing it for free, which was wonderful for Pamela, but it didn't give her or TrustDALE the satisfaction of restitution and preventing the auto shop from running this scam on someone else.

Even though this car rip-off had a happy ending due to AAMCO's generosity, that is not what normally happens. TrustDALE and its partners can't rescue and arrange for expensive pro bono services for every victim of the Rip-Off Range.

That is why I want you to understand the nature of scams and scammers—how they lure you in by creating a connection, establishing credibility, and playing on your emotions.

Hopefully, Pamela will never again take her car to an off-brand auto repair shop that takes no pride in its profession. The employees of Big Guy's not only charged her for services not rendered, ruined her car, and used her vehicle as their own, but (according to Pamela) they held her car hostage for an unreasonable amount of time. It's true that in most transactions, consumers must exercise some level of trust; after all, the company has what you want, so you have to take the first step—in Pam's case, giving them possession of her car. The next step is critical. Once you suspect you are being taken advantage of and not getting what you paid for, you need to explore ways to cut your losses and get out.

THE THREE EMOTIONAL ELEMENTS OF A SCAM

Never underestimate a scammer's intelligence. They are experts at using logical fallacies—errors in reasoning—as bait. They know, for instance, that emotion is the number-one driver of consumer behavior. Like Pavlov's dog, humans are eerily susceptible to following a familiar prompt, even when it harms them. In virtually every scenario, the prompts scammers use work because the consumer is pursuing an offer that's too good to be true. Foiling scammers requires not only knowledge of basic Scam Land behavior, but also the ability to curb our own greed, which we will learn more about later.

Here are the three common elements or emotional prompts scammers use to attract their victims.

1) They create a personal connection. What we may think of as networking, schmoozing, or kind inquiries are really part of the hunt when it comes to scammers. They strike up a conversation, asking where you're from (which by coincidence is near where they're from), noting a family member has your same name, or commenting on your food selection. Maybe they offer to help you with something: putting your luggage in the overhead bin on a plane, filling out a form. The goal is to create a bond that establishes this person is your ally; you both come from the same place or believe the same things.

This is exactly what Daniel Lemon did with Delia in the story at the beginning of this chapter. Once he claimed to be a friend of her son's, the path was open for him to sell her something that did not exist. If Delia had challenged that from the beginning, asking for some proof, her story would have a different ending.

2) They establish credibility. These con artists may claim to be from a real company or organization, directed to contact you to solve a problem. This could extend to the con presenting fake ID or credentials, but is most often conveyed through a phone call.

For instance, a man who claimed to be the "chief" in charge of the warrant division of a nearby county sheriff's department contacted me. He said he was calling to let me know an arrest warrant had been issued for my failure to appear in court for a traffic case. He claimed I'd been a witness to a traffic accident and had received a summons to testify. When I told him I was not and had not, he agreed with me, admitting they'd had a rash of mistaken identities. It's what he did next that tipped me off this was a total scam.

He advised that I could plow through the legal system and try to get the warrant dismissed while risking being "picked up," or I could come down to the sheriff's department and pay the $185 fine for failure to appear by placing the payment under a code he would provide in the kiosk found in the lobby. Then I was to take the receipt for the payment to the clerk's office where, under his emailed direction, I would immediately be issued a refund. Why would I go to all that trouble when I was not a witness and had not been notified to testify?

I used my connections with that county's sheriff's department to learn the call was a complete ruse, coordinated by scammers on both the outside and *inside* of the jail. When you deposit your money, preferably via gift card, it automatically goes into the account of an inmate!

Thousands fall for this scam all over the country every day, simply because a con man used the title "chief" to establish credibility. As humans living in a post-industrial society, we have been trained to defer to perceived authority figures, particularly those with titles connected to any helping profession or those with advanced degrees: police officers, the military, firefighters, doctors, lawyers, government officials. We have an emotional investment in believing that those who have sworn to take care of our health or uphold the law will do so. But people can say they are anything. Smart consumers will ask for proof of identification!

3) THEY PLAY ON YOUR EMOTIONS, often in combination with element one or two. Appealing to fear, joy, and sadness and using flattery, pity, and ridicule are age-old techniques to set someone up for a punch. Aristotle described emotional arousal as a necessary element of persuasion. Using an appeal to the emotions is very effective in convincing someone something is true when there is no evidence.

> *Appealing to fear, joy, and sadness and using flattery, pity, and ridicule are age-old techniques to set someone up for a punch.*

The grandmother of one of my colleagues at TrustDALE received a call late one night from a man claiming to be her grandson's attorney. The caller said her grandson was in jail for DUI and vehicular homicide. As luck would have it, he continued, the magistrate judge was "on the take," and for $2,000 the attorney could get her grandson released on bond. The attorney then told Grandma "Mikey" didn't want his parents to know and to please keep it private, and that's exactly what Grandma did.

This ninety-two-year-old woman followed the attorney's instructions to visit a Western Union location and wire the money to the destination he provided. After the first successful wire transfer, the "attorney" called back with bad news. "The judge says it's not enough. He wants $2,000 more." So Grandma made a trip to a different Western Union, as instructed.

Months went by with no word from Mikey. Grandma was sworn to silence. You can imagine her relief when she finally got to see him at a family reunion.

"Mikey, have you been to court yet?" she whispered.

"Grandma, I don't know what you're talking about," he responded.

After she recounted the phone call and her actions, Mikey said, "I promise I haven't been in jail and I haven't been in a car accident." Within minutes she was in tears, confessing her embarrassment to her children and grandkids.

After a long federal investigation, Western Union admitted in 2018 to aiding and abetting wire fraud, and agreed to pay $586 million in restitution to victims. Grandma filed a claim and is on the list for a refund. Check out TrustDALE.com for updates on whether she gets it. But know this: Grandma's outcome is not the rule, but a rare exception.

Grandmas are the most tenderhearted of targets for a scammer. But how much less stressful it would have been for Grandma if her loved ones had previously explained to her that she must never deliver money via any method to a stranger who offers no proof.

We think we live in a reasonable society where good is good and bad is bad. But we do not. Times and technology have changed, but not human nature.

There has never been a shortage of people willing to take on the risks of making "easy" money, as well as people who fall prey to their schemes. That's why consumers MUST be armed with the knowledge to make smart choices. The marketplace will always have its shady side.

Times and technology have changed, but not human nature.

The best way for consumers and even businesses, because they are consumers too, to save the billions of dollars a year wasted on scams is to not get scammed.

It may help to know that most famous scammers were unable to enjoy their fortunes. Many went to jail, some were shot by their former victims (not advised), and as poetic justice, others fell for scams themselves.

How did that happen, given their knowledge of scams? Because they were convinced they were smarter than everyone else.

Not true.

If each person who reads this book learns to avoid being taken in by these everyday tricksters, and passes on the lessons to others, it will make a difference. Once you recognize how to spot a scam, you will not be easily fooled again.

I believe it is most helpful to recognize the general characteristics of a scam. But you will find a list of what the FBI and I consider some of the most common cons in Appendix A.

THE ELEMENTS OF A SCAM

- **THE RIP-OFF RANGE** is an area of the economy in which scammers defraud consumers of significant amounts of money with few consequences as a result of loopholes and lack of communication between law enforcement and the courts.
- **THE EMOTIONAL ELEMENTS OF A SCAM** include creating a personal connection, establishing credibility, and playing on your emotions.

YOUR DEFENSIVE POSITION

Fast **_Funds_** **_Found_**
X X X

Define

Price
Offer
Product

Authenticate

References
Reviews
Reports

Ensure

Ethical
Equitable
Effective

Legitimize

License
Liability Insurance
Lawsuit/Background Check

YOUR OFFENSIVE APPROACH

CHAPTER 2

FAST FUNDS FOUND (FFF)

DALE'S CASE STUDY FILES
Moving Scam: Angie

Angie needed a mover to pick up and transport furniture from her one-bedroom condo in Atlanta to her new home in Florida. As most consumers do with almost every move, Angie underestimated the amount of "stuff" she had and thought she'd be able to get it all done for cheap. She called a couple of companies she found online and was stunned at the "ballpark" price range she was given over the phone.

Her next move took her past the point of no return. She saw a flyer tacked to a telephone pole near her home. It read: "Best Price, Peach State Moving and Storage." She dialed the number and scheduled an estimate. True to the posted flyer, Peach State told her they'd do the job for $1,244, almost 50 percent less than the estimates she'd received from the other companies. Angie produced her credit card and paid for half up front. The terms required her furniture be loaded only once into the same truck that would unload her furniture in Florida.

Angie's heart began to sink when, upon arrival, she saw her belongings start spilling out of a small moving van—not the truck that had left her Atlanta home several days before. She watched helplessly as two men she'd never met took no care at all in unloading her furniture and family heirlooms and proceeded to bang them on the ground and against the doors and walls of her new home.

Angie was furious, but it would only get worse. The two men insisted on final payment—in cash—before they unloaded her most precious possessions. Angie felt helpless. She went to the bank, withdrew the $622, and handed it over to the movers.

Angie was glad her contract required Peach State to compensate her for damages. Darius, the manager, told her they would take care of it and asked her to email photographs, which she did. They told her an insurance claim would be filed within days. Then, nothing. Peach State stopped taking her phone calls.

That's when Angie started doing the investigating she should have done before hiring the rogue mover. Here's what she learned.

Demand letters from her attorney were returned as undeliverable because Peach State had listed a fake street address. Her attorney also learned the company was not registered with the secretary of state. The final nail was discovering the company was not registered as a legitimate mover with the Department of Public Safety.

If Angie had only known prior to hiring Peach State Moving that every legitimate mover in her home state is required to register, and that consumers can actually file complaints that are tallied and displayed on the state's website, she would have known to steer clear.

Because she didn't know, Angie was out $1,244—until she reached out to TrustDALE. Our first advice to Angie was to challenge her up-front deposit with her credit card provider. It took a few months, but when her bank discovered her mover was illegitimate, they refunded Angie's deposit.

We scheduled an estimate of our own with Peach State Moving. Like a hungry wolf, the company jumped at the chance to make more money and showed up at the location we agreed upon over the phone. When Darius arrived, my team and I jumped out with cameras rolling. I never tire of this moment—I call it reeling in the shark. Darius jumped into his vehicle and sped away.

The next day, he agreed to close his rogue moving business and refund Angie the remainder of her payment—IF I didn't show his face and expose his name on my TV show. I agreed to the deal, because my goal was to make Angie whole. However, our radar is always up for fake movers, and so far, Darius appears to have found another line of work.

Angie had a positive outcome because she found TrustDALE. Sadly, most victims don't, so here's what we need to learn from Angie's experience. She made a decision—on the spot—with no research. Second, she believed the job could be performed for a price far less than true market value. Finally, she discovered too late that the company she hired could not be found. It's time to learn about Fast Funds Found.

As I said at the beginning of our journey, Fast Funds Found is like playing smart defense. The offer comes out of the blue, appeals to your emotions, and on the surface looks like a great opportunity. Here's a real-world example: You answer a knock at your door. A man in a crisp white uniform tells you he delivers meat for a high-end beef producer. Their product is usually reserved for the very best restaurants, but as luck would have it, he has a surplus right there in his refrigerated truck and his manager has authorized him to sell his choice steaks to a lucky resident along his route. What do you do? Fast Funds Found will remind you to 1) slow down and think, 2) not throw money at strangers, and 3) make sure whomever you do business with has a real name, address, and place of business. Let's go a little deeper.

Fast Funds Found

I'll bet you a box of hand-packed Georgia peaches that every time you have been taken in by a scam, spent more than you intended, or had buyer's remorse, you made your decision way too fast. Speed is an essential element of a successfully executed con.

Speed is an essential element of a successfully executed con.

Don's Tree Experts, serving clients in and around Stone Mountain, Georgia, has perfected the quick grab. When they come out to give you an estimate on tree trimming, tree cutting, or stump removal, they offer a discounted price if you sign on the dotted line and pay that day before they leave. If you wait, however, the price goes up.

Most people will sign up to get that discount. After all, they may have already been to the simple, but attractive, website for Don's Tree Experts that says they are a full-service company, family owned and operated with over forty years of experience. They call themselves a "second-generation tree service" because their expertise has been handed down from generation to generation. Furthermore, "We treat our customers with respect and conduct our work with the highest level of professionalism. We're passionate about the work we do, so you can rest assured that when you call us you're getting the top-notch service you expect."

Sounds great. But what's the rush with the discount offer?

If they give you more time, you might do more research or acquire more information that would reveal this company's services are rarely completed or finished within the agreed-upon time.

Deidra learned this the hard way. She paid $1,500 up front on the day of the estimate to get two hardwood trees cut down that were in danger of falling on her house. She waited to hear from a scheduler, but no one ever called. When she thought to check the Better Business Bureau website (bbb.org), she was blown away by what she discovered. Don's Tree Experts had a score of "F" and over two dozen complaints from customers who all had the same story: the work had not been done and the consumers were not able to get their money back.

After Deidra came to TrustDALE for help, we identified sixteen court cases against the owner of the business, Angela Hodges, and learned that she seemed to prey mostly upon older single black females. For the most part, the cases do not get settled because either she doesn't come to the hearing or, if she comes, the court will not serve her for other potential cases against her when she is physically in court, an odd "safe harbor" provision of Georgia law.

Rather than Don's Tree Experts being a second-generation business with forty years of experience, Hodges had only been in business since 2008. She must have added up all the years of experience of each staff member to come up with the number. In addition, although it says on materials they are fully licensed and insured, the business is only insured for landscaping, not tree removal. In fact, it turns out Hodges is essentially a broker who hires a company she claims is insured to cut down the trees. Potential clients sure would not get that idea based on what the website says.

As a result of TrustDALE's involvement, the DeKalb County, Georgia, police department issued warrants for Hodges' arrest. Whether Deidra will get her money back is questionable. But I doubt she will ever again jump at paying in advance for a deal that is available only during the limited time of an estimator's home visit. Making a fast decision on a deal means you don't have time to call a family member or friend, do an internet search, or just mull it over and see what your gut tells you. Of course, the amount of time needed to make an important decision varies with the value of the product, but I know of very few services I would purchase from a person who isn't willing to allow me twenty-four hours to make up my mind.

Fast Funds Found

Offering what appears to be an amazing windfall of money, grown on trees in a faraway place from someone you've never heard of, is an evergreen scam.

This may involve a large inheritance from a long-lost relative or wealthy benefactor—a dream come true for anyone who is debt-ridden or looking to elevate his or her lifestyle and image. The scammer poses as a lawyer, banker, or official who claims you are legally entitled to the money because you were tracked down as the next of kin, or someone who claims he or she can help you obtain a fortune left by someone with no will because you both have the same last name. All it will take to collect your money is some minor legal shenanigans.

You will be asked to provide personal details, like your bank account number for transfer of funds or your birth certificate and other ID. Then the agent will need fees for this and that, government regulations, taxes, etc. Then more money will be necessary, which will be repaid when your inheritance is deposited.

You will soon find there is no inheritance. Nor is there any way to get your money back.

Another version of this scam is awarding a prize to someone out of the blue. Robert was offered an opportunity to participate in a contest because "he was a valued customer of Best Buy." He was asked three simple questions, which he answered correctly, and was told he had won a $500 gift certificate to Best Buy. He verified some personal facts for the caller and was told to pick up the gift certificate at the nearest store the next Tuesday at 2:00 p.m.

Some of the personal information Robert gave the caller was his address and the fact that he lived alone. The next Tuesday, when he went to pick up his gift certificate, none of the employees at Best Buy knew what he was talking about.

At the same time he was trying to collect his prize, two men pulled up in front of his house in a van marked "Junk Removal" (spotted and reported after the fact by a neighbor). It took them ten minutes to break into his house and load the safe in his bedroom closet with $20,000 in cash, as well as other valuables and his gun collection, into their van and drive away.

Robert had been had by experts who knew how to bait a line and reel in the money.

> *Never respond to strangers who ask for up-front money in order to send you money, or who request personal information about your bank accounts, credit cards, or living arrangements.*

Never respond to strangers who ask for up-front money in order to send you money, or who request personal information about your bank accounts, credit cards, or living arrangements. If a computer is available when you receive a phone call, look up the contact details or exact wording of what is said, followed by a comma and the word "scam." Do the same thing with an email, especially if there are misspellings in the text. You can also use snopes.com as a fairly reliable source and type in the wording suggested above. Often a history of the scam pops up.

Fast Funds Found

If there's one thing scammers at large have in common, it's the desire to not be found. If you can't locate the person who took your money and promised you this, that, and the moon, you can't get your money back, you can't prosecute them or have them arrested, and you can't badmouth their business or ruin their reputation by name—both of which may have been fake anyway.

Some years ago a buddy of mine I worked with at the Nashville TV station fell victim to the "White Van Speaker Scam." He ought to have known better, but got caught up in the story a young man in a shopping-center parking lot told him. He explained that he was delivering speakers around town for a speaker-installation company. Since the company was overstocked (due to some vague glitch), and he had more than he was supposed to deliver, he had authorization to get rid of as much inventory as he could before returning to his base. He could offer my friend a great deal: only $250 for $1,000 high-quality, high-fidelity speakers.

By the time my friend got the speakers home, he had a funny feeling about this deal and researched the interaction he had in the parking lot. He found out what he had bought into was an organized, well-scripted enterprise that played out in parking lots and gas stations all over the country—in fact, all over the world. The targets were usually college students who looked affluent or foreigners who weren't familiar with typical business transactions in Western countries and were perhaps used to bargaining with individuals.

Sure enough, when my friend tried to hook the speakers up, the bass worked but the woofer and tweeter were fake. They were worth about $50.

Values vary in this sham, but the logistics are the same. Distributors rent a warehouse and obtain licenses and distribution rights, then import large quantities of inferior goods, shipping them to local warehouses in major cities where a sales team has been trained to work off a script. Contact details are false and the vehicles used are leased and cannot be traced.

Years later I had an opportunity to bust one of these operations on TV. They had a little office where they all gathered in the morning, had their power drinks, and did a group cheer before going out to rip people off. Then they came back and counted their money.

Friends, get to know your merchant or service provider. Do they have a website? Is there an "About Us" section that identifies

They had a little office where they all gathered in the morning, had their power drinks, and did a group cheer before going out to rip people off. Then they came back and counted their money.

the owners and employees? Does their address pan out when you check the location? Be careful, crooks have found ways to cut and paste fake storefronts onto search engine maps. See if that office corresponds with their address filed with your secretary of state. Do they have a Facebook or LinkedIn page? The more extensive their identifiable network is, the better.

As an experiment during the holiday season, TrustDALE tested how easy it would be to scam the public out of money during the holidays. I asked one of my coworkers to dress up like Santa and sit at an intersection with a red bucket. In four hours he collected hundreds of dollars because people assumed, or wanted to believe, that someone in a Santa suit with a red bucket was there for a good cause. It was easy to mistake him for a Salvation Army Santa in front of a store—except he didn't have a Salvation Army sign or the official red kettle, and he wasn't in front of a store.

Of course, we gave the money to a certified charity. But I am concerned that people are so trusting and big-hearted they will give money to a random dude in a costume, just because they think he needs it. He didn't even have a handwritten sign that said he was homeless. These are the same people who are taken in by **Fast Funds Found**.

If you don't insist on the time to ask questions and get answers before rushing into a deal, you are moving too fast. If you jump at the chance to claim funds, your greed will not be rewarded; in fact, you will lose money. If you don't demand proof that the person offering you a deal is who he says he is with a findable business address and legitimate contact information, you may very well be left in the dark with nothing to show for your efforts to save money.

Remember the knock at the door from the man in the crisp white uniform earlier in this chapter? It's a scam that's worked for years across the US. After spending hundreds of dollars for choice steaks, the unsuspecting consumer discovers that the beef is either spoiled or regular supermarket grade. At this point, the salesperson is long gone, and yes, can't be found.

These first three steps do not require a big investment of time or resources. Simply remember Fast Funds Found, or FFF, to put on the brakes before you smash into a high curb on a curve.

FAST FUNDS FOUND

- **Fast Funds Found** are the first three steps to becoming a savvy consumer. Do not be tricked into making a fast decision, believing a stranger or company will give you unearned funds, or not requiring authentic evidence of an individual or company's contact information.

CHAPTER 3

DEFINE YOUR DEAL

D E A L

DALE'S CASE STUDY FILES
Locked Up by a Locksmith: Garrett

Garrett Anderson was at a Walmart when he locked his keys in the car. He looked for a nearby locksmith on his phone and called the first one, G-A Lock and Key. He was told someone would be there in fifteen minutes, and that the fee would be $75; but he did not get the name of the dispatcher or any information on where the locksmith was coming from. He waited for forty-five minutes.

The fact that he had to wait so long indicates the business he called might be a scam. Crooks know that if you have invested fifteen minutes, you will wait another thirty, and so on. They figure they have an hour to get to you. A reputable company will keep in touch with the customer and let them know the ETA, calling back with any changes.

When locksmith Tanzu Kanlica got to the parking lot and unlocked the car, Garrett learned the $75 quoted on the phone was the fee for coming out. There was an unlock charge that was also $75.

Because Garrett did not have $150 on him, the locksmith said he would follow him to an ATM.

So far, this has all the signs of a Fast Funds Found shakedown. Neither the time nor the fee was quoted accurately, indicating customer service satisfaction was not a priority. Then when the locksmith arrived, Garrett assumed he knew the elements of the deal without asking questions and requiring written confirmation. In addition, the person who arrived was not in a truck with the business's name on it—never a good sign—but in a silver Nissan 350Z.

Garrett nervously agreed to go to an ATM about two miles from Walmart. Law enforcement later testified a chase ensued. On the way to the ATM, the locksmith lost control of his car and killed two girls and injured a third. Because Garrett was ahead and did not know what had happened behind him, he drove home when he became aware Kanlica's Nissan was no longer following him.

Later that night the Cobb County police arrested Garrett for vehicular homicide, and for not paying the locksmith.

Wait! What?

The locksmith agreed to plead guilty to vehicular homicide and to testify against Garrett. He testified Garrett was well aware the accident had happened, that he saw it and left the scene.

When the locksmith and his boss were on the stand, they were asked about their pricing model because it was the crux of Garrett's motive to lose the locksmith on his tail so he would not have to pay.

Because they are roving wolves when it comes to catching innocent prey, the locksmiths spoke from a script that had been used a million times and lied on the stand about how they priced a job. Garrett might as well have been a butterfly in a hurricane.

Garrett has spent the last four *years* in jail and is fighting for a new trial, but so far the court will not commute his sentence. The locksmith is serving a jail sentence as well. But the owner of the company, Yagel Gabriel Amram, who was responsible for the corrupt scams this company, and others he owns, runs on consumers every day, is still free. See my TrustDALE investigative report online at TrustDALE.com/tdi.

This is perhaps one of the saddest cases I have ever come across. Garrett was sucked into a scam so beyond his control he ended up in jail for a crime he did not commit. Reasonable people would think he could just pay the locksmith and be done with the legal end of this nightmare. And that the locksmith company would be locked down, knocked down, and abandoned in shame. In the absence of the imaginary consumer police in our minds, this was not the case. It was business as usual for the bad guys.

How could such a terrible thing happen? An innocent motorist was framed for an accident that caused deaths and injuries by a driver and car he wasn't even near.

This is an extreme example of the vileness of humans who are out to make a buck on your back. Without getting into a debate about the politics and legal strategies that may have been involved in this case, let's examine how Garrett could have protected himself.

According to AAA, about four million people lock their keys in their car every year. The best thing Garrett could have done for himself is to have had an automobile club membership card in his wallet so he could have called a company with a great reputation for rescuing stranded motorists, a company that works with mechanics and service stations they trust all over the country. If you have a car or your kids drive a car, consider membership in AAA or a comparable automobile club, or check beforehand to see if your auto policy covers locksmiths and in what amount.

Garrett had not defined an important need in regard to how he traveled around every day: access to quick and reliable help should anything go wrong with his car.

First, lacking an automobile club "rescue plan," Garrett should have checked the reviews on G-A Lock and Key, the company that came up first on his phone. If he had, he would have seen they were very bad, and perhaps gone to the next locksmith, checking their reviews, too, before calling to request help. Not identifying the quality or characteristics of the locksmith before calling left him open to being scammed.

Second, when Garrett was quoted the price and time for getting his car unlocked, he didn't ask enough questions—the majority of us don't. He didn't pin down what the $75 was for and under what conditions there would be additional costs. He didn't call back or ask for the driver's number so he could monitor his progress.

Third, Garrett didn't take the time, and I'm sure he was being rushed as part of the "script" this company follows to trap their victims, to insist on an up-front final quote, through either text or email, or presented in writing upon arrival and prior to the unlock.

Garrett is no different than the typical consumer. The outcome of his trust, however, was so severe that I want to be sure everyone who finishes this book is skeptical enough to follow through with every step of my acronyms FFF and DEAL. If you do, I guarantee your chances of being scammed like Garrett are slim to none. But, to be honest, I want them to be ZERO!

It's time to move into the proactive portion of this book. This is where your offensive strategy will come into play, and I've outlined four steps to help you put it in action: DEAL. When you're seeking out a product or service, you can use DEAL to measure the most important elements involved. DEAL will help you know enough about the subject matter to keep you on the path to a smart purchase:

- **Define your deal** by identifying the product, offer, and price.
- **Ensure your deal** by insisting on ethical negotiation, an equitable contract, and an effective guarantee.
- **Authenticate your deal** by researching references, reviews, and reports on the company or individual.
- **Legitimize your deal** by requiring proof of licensing, liability insurance, and past lawsuits the company or individual may have been involved in.

With DEAL in your toolbox, you'll be equipped to challenge scammers head on. If you think learning how to be a savvy consumer is too hard because you have to do "homework," think of it this way: you only have to learn these steps once, yet they will save you money for the rest of your life. Let's get started.

First, you'll take the time to **define** your needs by exploring and understanding the **product**, comparing **offers**, and then determining **price**. Doing so involves nothing more than the basic critical-thinking skills I advocate teaching in middle school. After all, adult life as a wage earner involves one purchase after another, each one with variables that differentiate a successful transaction of money well spent from a negative experience of money down the drain. Adolescents are at the perfect age for consumer training because they are motivated by cultural cues to buy the latest products companies push as a trend. To them, their desires are indistinguishable from needs. They want what they want now. And they do not yet know enough about the big bad world of false advertising, marketing scams, and outright rip-offs.

What you're looking for in a product or service is *quality*. Take, for example, the quest for the best vacuum cleaner. You want to understand where different brands rank in terms of quality of design, practicality, and durability. These are things you can read about, eyeball, and calculate with a hands-on experience.

But the first step is to define what you want.

PERSON A: Wants powerful suction for removing pet hair, and a steam-cleaning option for removing stains and spills from carpeting.

PERSON B: Wants a roaming vacuum that cleans for an hour or more on its own and can go under a table and chairs. It should keep the floor spotless so the house is ready for surprise visitors and can accommodate toddler grandchildren who might ingest something off the floor.

> *TIP: Write down the qualities or options you want.*
> *Don't just say it, see it.*

After defining what you want in general, often idealistic, terms, define what it is that you need.

Person A: Needs a more sanitary environment because of a family member with allergies, so powerful suction is extremely important. They also need to stay within a budget. Steam-cleaning is less important, as stains can be attacked by hand individually, or a service can come in occasionally or for emergencies.

> *TIP: After analyzing offer and price on the most powerful suction vacuums, price the annual cost for carpet-cleaning services. If you bought a vacuum with powerful suction and a steam-cleaning element, would it save you money considering the price of carpet cleanings throughout the year?*

Person B: Needs a roaming vacuum cleaner because does not have time to regularly push vacuum due to working fulltime and over-committing to volunteer and social activities; money is not an issue but service is, because reliability is paramount to saving time.

> *TIP: Pay attention to getting a comprehensive guarantee for convenient service or a quick replacement.*

This will be your basic blueprint to refer to when in doubt. Too many people lose sight of what they were looking for in the first place once they are subjected to high-pressure sales tactics, too-good-to-believe offers, or a heavily discounted price that skimps in other areas (like powerful suction). That's when you end up with a product or service that doesn't meet your criteria, which leads to buyer's remorse and other unpleasant consequences. A penny saved on something you don't want is not worth a cent.

DEFINE YOUR **PRODUCT**

It's easier to narrow down and **define the product** or service after you've decided what you need. First, talk to your friends and/or others about what you're looking for and ask them what they like or dislike about—to continue the example above—the brand of vacuum they have. Ask to borrow the best option and try it out in your own home. Most people will be willing to loan something out for an agreed-upon time limit if you're a reliable person and can reciprocate the favor in some other way. This may take as little as an hour, but should never last more than two days, since it is an inconvenience.

Second, visit stores and become familiar with the brands. Target and Walmart carry at least a half dozen different vacuums. Although you can compare features and prices online (with the added bonus of having your purchase delivered to your door), it is still helpful to examine products in person. You can get the feel of the weight and ease of movement of different brands and inspect the quality of the material.

Do not discount visiting specialty stores like Dyson, Hoover, Oreck, and Kirby (which involve a home demonstration rather than an in-store experience). Specialty brands are also available secondhand or refurbished via eBay and Craigslist. Before making a deal on a higher-end appliance, though, you should definitely ask for a demonstration and a hands-on tryout. Remember that you most likely will not be getting a guarantee with a used product, so you will have to weigh the discounted price against the possibility of service or replacement fees that might add up to the cost of a brand-new vacuum.

You do the same thing whether you're shopping for a product or a service.

Let's say you are looking for a cleaning service. You know the first step: define and write down what you want and need.

PERSON A: Wants a cleaning service to come twice a month on Fridays so more time can be spent relaxing.

PERSON B: Wants a reliable person to come into the home two to three times a week to clean the house, do laundry, and keep up with window washing and other occasional maintenance.

First, talk with others who use a service to find out who they use and why they chose a particular company or person. Search the internet for options and look them up on reputable sites like TrustDALE, or seek opinions on the free community website Nextdoor.

Second, set up an interview. If you use TrustDALE, there is no need for an interview. But for anything else, set up phone or in-person interviews to discuss product, offer, and price.

DEFINE YOUR **OFFER**

I began this chapter with a tragic tale. Individuals and companies who use tricks or gimmicks—or entrapment—to sell their products are better at understanding human nature than creating a value proposition. They are experts at their craft. It is delusional to think you can outsmart a con game if you have not been educated on how to protect yourself and your assets. Here is what you need to know in order to **define the offer**.

First, recognize that offers like the "clearance sale" are intended to trigger an emotional reaction. What it should be called is the "inventory we couldn't sell when it was in season and therefore it is truly worth less" trick. Likewise, the "50 percent off sale" is usually just a gimmicky way of saying, "We cut a falsely inflated price by 50 percent to make you believe we're selling it half-price." As a consumer investigator, I find these types of discount gimmicks obvious, overdone, and ridiculous. They persist, however, because of one undeniable fact. They are effective. In fact, one of our unofficial national holidays is Black Friday, the day after Thanksgiving when Christmas gifts (or any product for any time) are deeply discounted. This day in November has turned into such a frantic competition that people have been injured shopping.

Public perception is that merchants are discounting their most popular items by 50 percent or more that one day. While many companies do accept a smaller profit margin in exchange for a very high volume for one day, the reality is this: an entire industry has emerged that produces lower-cost and even substandard knock-offs for high-demand products. An example is that name-brand TV. Would you be as anxious to purchase it if you knew the factory had intentionally produced a Black Friday run of TVs that carried fewer components than the ones advertised in non–Black Friday circulars?

Second, recognize that if the offer is so time-dependent that you're rushed through a decision, you're not headed for quality at a fair price; you're headed for an ambush. Don't fall for that.

Sellers who want you to decide on the basis of a stopwatch believe you are vulnerable to taking something of lesser quality or higher cost in exchange for a perceived discount. A car salesperson might work on your dreams to get you to agree to a more expensive car offered at a discount if you buy it right then, without allowing you time to look at the mechanics yourself or bring a friend to assess its quality. A condo salesperson who offers a free weekend trip if you sit through a talk on buying a condo is trained to talk you into buying something you had no intention of purchasing when you agreed to take the free trip. They go by a script that has an answer or response for every objection or concern you might raise.

Creating urgency prevents consumers from examining the offer, comparing prices, and discussing the purchase with other people. That's why you need to go through your defining process before you face subtle harassment by agents who are only thinking about their commissions.

When my wife was pregnant with our first child, we were twenty-five years old and green as gourds. A baby furniture store invited us to a free demonstration of a pram, which I learned was a fancy word for a baby carriage, with the incentive of a gift certificate to a restaurant. The two hours we spent learning about that extraordinary pram were filled with the most aggressive, hard sell I have ever experienced.

This pram could do everything ten ways to Sunday. This wasn't just a mode of transportation. It accommodated a car seat so you didn't have to wake the baby when moving from place to place. It folded down into a bed and up into a more traditional stroller. It had storage for everything from a diaper bag to a cup of coffee and for extra blankets and jackets. It could accommodate a bag or two of groceries.

We were impressed by its versatility, but it was $2,000. We came very close to purchasing the pram on a credit card, for which we would have ended up paying hundreds of dollars or more in interest. As I was leaving the presentation, I told the energetic salesman I would have to think about it overnight. Suddenly tired, he said, "You won't be back." He knew if I had the strength to walk away from that hard sell, he would not get me back. Time was of the essence in roping me in.

> TIP: *Whenever time is of the essence in sealing a deal, do not take the bait. Back away, or you will be hooked. More people have regrets about what they did buy than what they didn't.*

The third consideration when comparing offers is to be sure to read the mice type on the screen or paper. Forgetting your magnifying glasses is not an excuse. You MUST know what you are signing up for before agreeing to a contract or purchase; otherwise, how can you properly gauge its value?

In a cautionary tale with a completely positive spin, a teacher of life skills at a Georgia high school recently won $10,000 from a travel insurance company solely for reading the fine print. Donelan Andrews was seven pages into the paperwork issued by the Florida-based company Squaremouth for a policy named Tin Leg when she spotted this sentence: "If you've read this far, then you are one of the very few Tin Leg customers to review all their policy documentation." The company had run a secret contest with a $10,000 reward to the first person to respond. Andrews responded only twenty-three hours after the event launched.

In all fairness, she did have an advantage in that she has a consumer economics background and teaches students in all of her classes the importance of reading a contract. Her win could not be more to the point in illustrating how essential that skill is. This one time, she netted a reward. But other times, she may very well have lost money if she had not read the fine print.

DEFINE YOUR **PRICE**

Only after you've explored products and compared offers can you accurately measure price. The internet has revolutionized our ability to research price, but it seems no amount of insight into what something "ought" to cost can diminish our desire to get a "deal." You know, a deal is something your neighbor gets on his brand-new car. A deal is that reduction your coworker got on her brand-new laptop. What they're probably not telling you is what they gave up to get that deal—maybe because they don't recognize that factor themselves.

Your neighbor may have gotten 0 percent financing, but he agreed to make payments for eight years on a car that will be worth far less than his remaining payments by year five. Your coworker may have gotten a deal on that laptop, but she agreed to a hefty protection package that will expire just before her hard drive conks out. The simple fact is our economy operates on supply and demand. The more people want it, the more they'll pay. The less people want it, well, you know.

The first thing you must do when it comes to **defining the price** you are willing to pay for a service or product is to take emotion out of the equation. Erase the image of yourself in a red convertible driving by your friends who are staring at you stunned. Remember, scammers and con artists will try to engage your emotions, so deal with that issue ahead of time.

For instance, before you go to a dealership, decide on (define) the make, model, and color you want. Then find a friend, or friend of a friend, who already has one and ask if you can drive it (just like in the vacuum cleaner example). You can even leave a note on a similar-model car in the parking lot of a place you frequent, asking the owner to contact you about whether they've been satisfied with the car's performance.

In addition, know it is almost always smarter to buy a used car. New cars depreciate by thousands of dollars the moment they are driven off the lot. That will help you detach from succumbing to the picture of yourself in a new car you never planned to buy.

The second thing to tackle is to compare prices. That means comparing apples to apples, not oranges. Product prices can vary considerably based on a small difference. Don't compare the price of a gold 2016 Toyota Camry to a white 2016 Toyota Camry. Some of the differential may be attributed to the popularity of gold or white. So start with researching what car color is the least and most expensive in general, and then decide how important color is to your choice.

Similarly, if you are considering buying a diamond ring, make a checklist of factors you and the marketplace consider important. Perform an internet search for "factors that affect diamond prices." Educate yourself on the variation in prices of gold, silver, white gold, and platinum bands and decide if you could settle for a less expensive band if you got the quality of diamond you want. Do the same process of discovery regarding diamond ring designs: given the same carat of diamond, how do design prices vary?

> *TIP: As you compare prices online, try not to be distracted by pop-up offers that come flying onto your screen before you have gathered information. These are distractions aimed at FOMO (Fear of Missing Out). Don't let these offers take you off the path to what you really need to find out.*

Getting estimates for services is the equivalent of comparing prices for products. The generally accepted practice is to get three estimates from three vendors. I don't agree. My advice is if the product or service costs $50 or less, do your comparisons online. If the cost is $200 or less and requires a visit to your home, get three estimates. If the cost is $500 or more, get more than three estimates. And if the cost is in the thousands, get as many estimates as it takes until you feel comfortable you've identified the fair market price. That way you can not only compare pricing, but also customer service, guarantees, warranties, repair expenses, the whole package. We will discuss separating real guarantees from worthless paper in chapter 4.

> TIP: Don't hesitate to inform sellers you're getting a number of estimates. A magical thing happens when contractors for services know they are competing against other businesses: the price comes down.

My friend and colleague, nationally syndicated radio host, consumer advocate, and best-selling author Clark Howard, has made a career out of saving money by appearing to be cheap. His tips on good buys aren't really based on what's least expensive, but on what delivers the best value. If you're looking for cheap, fast food, his research and experience have taught him the "best" cheap, fast food to recommend.

In the end, remember that price is just a number. The important thing is the value the consumer receives from the purchase. As legendary investor Warren Buffett has said, "Price is what you pay, value is what you get."

That is what this chapter is about: understanding value based on factors that are personal to you, the individual consumer. Once you have some experience making educated choices, these routines will become second nature, because the best way to save money is to get the most value for your money.

DEFINE YOUR DEAL

- **DEFINE** exactly what you want, whether a product or service, then narrow it down to need.
- **DEFINE YOUR PRODUCT** or service by getting

recommendations from friends and others, study-ing and ranking brands or companies, visiting stores to try the product, or making an in-home appointment for an interview and tryout.

- **DEFINE YOUR OFFER** by recognizing which dis-counts are gimmicks, realizing when you're being pressured to make a quick decision, and reading and understanding everything in print before signing any papers, contracts, or work orders.

- **DEFINE YOUR PRICE** by detaching from your emo-tions, comparing prices or estimates using the same or similar variables, and understanding the value of the product or service relative to its price.

CHAPTER 4

ENSURE YOUR DEAL

D E A L

DALE'S CASE STUDY FILES
Where Did My Car Go?: Tanqunika

Any time you buy a car without seeing it in person, there is likely to be trouble. But with a nightshift job and four children to transport to school, Tanqunika was desperate to find a large, safe, and cheap vehicle. She took a chance on a 2004 Lincoln Aviator—a luxury mid-sized SUV—advertised for sale by orderanycar.com.

The current site, orderanycars.com (plural of car), says all the right things: it represents licensed automobile dealers who offer dealer prices for cash purchases. Buyers will save $2,000 on average, and prices are comparable to trade-in values listed in the Kelley Blue Book.

Tanqunika spoke with the broker for over a month. She was told that the unbelievably low price she was quoted was even under the dealer price. That, of course, is a flaming red flag. But her relationship with the broker reassured Tanqunika that all would be well. Transactions are supposed to be speedy: complete seven days after money is deposited and signed documents are received.

Tanqunika should have noticed the warning signs from the very beginning. The broker wanted $4,725, which included a $350 broker fee, all of which Tanqunika deposited into the bank account of orderanycar.com. The next thing she knew, she was sent a photo of the 2004 Lincoln Navigator she now owned. However, that was not the car she had agreed to purchase, nor the car she wanted to own.

Tanqunika came to TrustDALE because she wasn't getting anywhere with orderanycar by herself, and she needed transportation.

TrustDALE followed the trail left by the owner of orderanycar. com, Curena Stones. We found no one at her address and only an empty, stripped office at her supposed place of business. We finally tracked her down by discovering she had been arrested by the local sheriff's department in another county and charged with theft by conversion, which could mean stealing money that had been sent to her to purchase a vehicle that was never delivered, although we have no hard evidence.

Stones did not have the Aviator Tanqunika purchased. This was a classic bait-and-switch scam that happens in car sales lots all over the country. The business advertises a specific car for an extremely low price to get people to drive to their lot and look at other cars that need to be sold. Consumers who are ready to buy will usually settle for something similar, but more costly or of less quality, even though it is not what they really wanted. This is illegal in most states now, but it is still practiced as an effective sales tactic.

Stones finally told me where the car in the picture she sent Tanqunika was located, and Oh My! it was in pitiful condition. It had been parked on the side of a road under a tree for a year. The tires were flat and it was not roadworthy. It was, by any defini-tion, a "lemon." The idea that Tanqunika would accept this sub-stitute for the car in the original picture was farfetched, but con artists count on dealing with people who are desperate for what-ever they can get when it comes to having something or nothing.

Once again, I asked TrustDALE's certified partner AAMCO if they could do a community service for this single mom who needed a safe vehicle for work and for transporting her children—which they did with generosity and humility. AAMCO hauled the car to one of their locations, performed an extensive systems check, and then repaired or replaced every failed component. AAMCO's ser-vice manager did not rest until, as he put it, "I would feel just as safe with the SUV if my wife was behind the wheel." Tanqunika was thrilled. See the story at TrustDALE.com/aamco.

An interesting note: The current site for this business is order-anycars.com. Evidently, Curena Stones changed the name of her company by adding an "s." She registered as the agent for order-anycars.com in 2018, and probably deleted the old site, which no longer pops up under orderanycar.com. That is one way of evading dissatisfied consumers, and the law—change the name of your business.

It is clear Tanqunika did not **ensure** she was getting a good deal by insisting on **ethical negotiation**, an **equitable contract**, and an **effective guarantee**. She did not yet know about my **DEAL** acro-nym. However, the biggest red flag of all, from the beginning, was that the car was priced far below its value as presented in the picture of the Lincoln Aviator, and presumably as portrayed by Curena Stones. Believing you have found a bargain that defies logic is a direct avenue to Scam Land.

TIP: That smug feeling you have when you think you've snagged an impossible bargain is almost always followed by the realization you've been taken for a ride.

Smart consumers accept that a good deal is a win-win for both consumer and seller. The consumer must pay a fair price so the seller can make a reasonable profit. If the price is too high, the consumer loses and the seller wins. If the price is too low, the consumer wins but the seller loses. Neither is a reasonable business model to sustain a free-market economy. Put on the brakes and assess the situation before committing to a purchase or signing a contract when something seems too good to be true.

> *Put on the brakes and assess the situation before committing to a purchase or signing a contract when something seems too good to be true.*

Excellence generally costs more—that includes quality of product and delivery of honest service. The money you spend up front will prove its worth in the end. Similarly, the time you put into **ensuring your deal is ethical, equitable, and effective** will also prove its worth. The value of ensuring these things is setting up a deal that will be safe, secure, and successful. You are protecting yourself from harm.

I am hoping Tanqunika will never again pay in advance for something as significant as a car, that she will thoroughly investigate the company or individual from whom she is making a large purchase, and that she will acknowledge and accept that when a price is too good to be true, it is.

ENSURE **ETHICAL NEGOTIATION**

Earlier in my consumer-reporting career, a woman I will call Laura called me for help with restitution for a car she had purchased at a third less than its market value. She was thrilled, until she went to register it with the state and discovered it was a salvage car. In fact, it was actually two cars in one. There was no way she could get insurance on it. The man from whom she bought the car had defrauded her.

This was not an **ethical negotiation** on several levels. First of all, the seller represented himself as the owner of the car, but was actually a car broker. This is called curbstoning. It usually involves a car dealer posing as a private seller in order to evade city or state regulations on authorized automobile sales. Dishonest dealers or brokers buy salvaged or flood-damaged cars at auction and then try to sell them to private buyers without disclosing the damage. As professional car flippers, they often have the technical ability to alter odometer settings and mask other serious problems.

The regulations that apply to car titles vary from state to state, presenting an irresistible opportunity for dishonest curbstoners. Laura's car had been purchased in another state, where the regulations were different. This is called title washing. A professional con artist can also physically alter a car's title through manipulating a new, official-looking document, or simply reapply for a new title without disclosing the car's history.

As with Tanqunika's car issue, the flapping red flag was the low price of the car offered to Laura. She charged forward with visions of sugar plums dancing in her head, as if it were Christmas Eve. But the fabulous gift she hoped to receive came from someone she did not know whose credentials she had not vetted.

> TIP: Be especially wary of personal ads selling used cars. If the seller asks "Which car?", chances are it's a curbstoner. Not too many individuals would have more than one vehicle to sell.

In any negotiation, you must ASK QUESTIONS AND VERIFY ANSWERS. Here is how Laura and Tanqunika could have **ensured their negotiation was ethical.**

Any used car has surely been to a mechanic at some point. An honest and responsible seller, whether they're a private owner or licensed dealer, should be able to provide you with service records, so do not hesitate to ask. Most curbstoners, and irresponsible private owners, will have nothing to show. In addition, search the internet for the contact phone number and email. If either comes up with a long list of car ads, you are most likely dealing with a curbstoner, not an individual trying to sell his or her personal property.

Contact your insurance agent for help to find out if there were any insurance claims paid on the vehicle you are considering. There is a national database that insurance companies have access to. However, if you are dealing with two vehicles that were totaled and then put together, this tactic will not give you the whole picture.

You can also use a service like Carfax to run a background check on the car, which will show salvage history, odometer problems, and if a rental or lease company used the vehicle. Carfax states, however, that it does not have a complete history of every vehicle.

A tactic my neighbor's father used for every car he purchased was to pay his mechanic a small amount to look at the car and offer an assessment of what was wrong or suspicious—and what was right, of course.

In Laura's case, she sued the seller in magistrate court (formerly small claims court), which should have been a slam dunk. In this case the broker avoided a judgment by not showing up in court the first few times, which is a delay tactic to get the complaint dismissed out of frustration. After my TV station pursued the broker, he did show up the next time, but to no avail for the consumer.

Something consumers may not know is that magistrate court judges are not necessarily attorneys familiar with the law. They are appointed officials. There were clearly grounds for the consumer to be refunded the full amount of her purchase for the car, but because the judge was not familiar with the law, the judge told them to leave the courtroom and not come back until they had negotiated a reasonable settlement, which was impossible. You cannot come to a reasonable settlement with an unprincipled seller.

That is why it's so important to **ensure** you are dealing with someone who is **ethical**. And to know the signs of a scam. If your counterpart in a negotiation does not share your commitment to a standard of conduct based on right and wrong (it is wrong to cover up past damage to a car; it is expected that both parties will be honest and transparent), you are positioned to lose your investment.

ENSURE AN **EQUITABLE CONTRACT**

To illustrate how tricky it is to **ensure your deal is equitable**, meaning it's fair to all, let me give you a down-to-earth example that happens every day in Downtown Atlanta. There is a long-running parking lot scam right here in Atlanta across from a federal building. The line to get into the lot is often long, so when a person walks up to your car and says he didn't use all his time and you can buy his used ticket for five dollars instead of waiting in line to pay twenty, many people pull out their wallets. When they return from their business, however, there may be a boot on their wheel. The attendant will say you didn't purchase a parking ticket. You will say you did, and it's clearly visible on the dash.

You may not think of a ticket as a contract, but actually it is. When you buy and display it in your car, you are agreeing to the rules and regulations printed on the ticket. If you had read the back of the ticket, you would know that tickets are not transferable. It's no use to argue with the parking lot attendant, because he's already in on the scam. The police know about their little sideline but won't get involved because it is a victimless crime. What happened to you happened because you were impatient and greedy.

Watch out for deals that are not **equitable** (in this case, a discounted ticket was clearly not a win-win for both parties). Win-lose or lose-win deals will bite you where you're tender—in your bank account. Safeguard your funds by being smart about when it's unwise to assume you can trust the world and its gatekeepers. It is as much your responsibility to ensure an equitable contract as it is the other party's.

I have two termite stories that illustrate inequitable contracts. Most homeowners think of their "termite bond" as both a maintenance contract and an insurance policy. It is actually a warranty between a consumer and a termite company that generally includes an agreement for termite inspections as long as the contract lasts, an agreement to provide treatment and control if termites are discovered, and an agreement to repair damages if a home qualifies, plus retreatment to prevent future damage. Bonds are often passed from one homeowner to another in the course of a house's history.

Jodi called TrustDALE after discovering termite damage in her recently purchased property, and that her termite bond was basically worthless. The house had been under a termite bond since

1983. At some point the little critters had gotten into the load-bearing beams, leaving them at risk of collapsing. The inspector from the termite company, which had held the bond for thirty-five years, told Jodi they were not responsible for any of the damage because the contract stated if there were no live termites in the wood, the company was not financially responsible for repairs.

This is actually considered standard language by many companies, so read your termite bond carefully and insist that the termite company keep up with maintenance checks and bait stations. If the company's policy is not to repair or replace damage, insist on rewriting the contract or find another company.

> *If the company's policy is not to repair or replace damage, insist on rewriting the contract or find another company.*

Once TrustDALE got involved, the house was reinspected and the company agreed to repair the damage because "that was the right thing to do." But there was no mention of doing the right thing until an outside force that could have embarrassed the company came into the picture. Go to, or threaten to go to, social, print, or TV media sites with your case if you have to. It's best to have an equitable contract in place from the beginning. But in a case like this, where a bond was passed along with the house for years, a little nudge from TrustDALE pushed the termite company into damage control. No company wants to be featured on the internet or TV for letting down loyal, long-term clients.

In another case of termite damage, a company came out and said they would replace only the portion of the hardwood floor that was damaged. The homeowners were dismayed because that part of the floor wouldn't match the rest. They came to a compromise in which the termite company would pay to sand the entire floor so the difference in wood was not so obvious.

But in this case, as in the previous one, the terms of replacement in case of damage were buried in the contract. Employees at these companies are trained not to reveal everything the contract says. So either get out those magnifying glasses and read every word yourself, or ask specific questions about replacement damage and insist on being guided to the language in the contract that pertains to that issue.

I am not an attorney, but I've seen many examples of bad agreements and have been asked hundreds of times how to proceed when considering a contract. The following is not legal advice, but a layman's guide for when you simply don't want to worry day and night over how to approach an agreement and when to get professional assistance.

It's my experience that contracts with a value of $100 or less can be placed on a single page and don't necessarily require expert review, although it's never a bad idea to have a wise set of eyes take a look. If the contract carries a value between $100 and $500, I would suggest running it by a friend who has expertise in the field, and make certain you or they have a thorough understanding of the opportunities and obligations contained in the document. If the agreement requires a payment between $500 and $1,000, consider paying a field expert a small fee (perhaps 5 percent of the contract value) to perform a review. Depending on your comfort level, this model can also work for obligations up to $5,000. The problem is, if your expert misses something, there's little you can do. If you want to minimize risk, my advice is to hire an attorney to review anything with an obligation of $5,000 or more. For a lawyer's perspective on how to approach contracts and when to hire an attorney, see my friend Barry Selvidge's thoughts in "When and How to Review a Contract or Agreement."

WHEN AND HOW TO
REVIEW A CONTRACT OR AGREEMENT

Contracts and agreements are facts of life. There are contractual requirements related to virtually every transaction you make—and you may not even realize it.

Stop and think how many times you agree to accept a website's privacy policy and terms and conditions without reading or even thinking about it. Not a problem—until it is. Which, for the most part, is never, but you have to be able to gauge the importance of things you agree to on a daily basis. You don't need a lawyer for agreeing to the terms of a website, but when *do* you need a lawyer?

Attorney and entrepreneur Barry Selvidge, with Newport LLC, shared these observations with me for this book. Since he was instrumental in helping me set up my TrustDALE business, he is a member of TrustDALE's community of trust I can vouch for.

First, do a "triage" process, Barry suggests. How important is your contract or agreement? The answer depends on several things: the amount of money involved, whether you have any negotiating leverage, and how long the contract is.

A $100,000 contract would rise to the top end of the scale as far as being reviewed by an attorney. A $1,000 or under contract (you have to set the amount depending on your financial position) would be lower on the scale of necessity. Related to price is the importance you place upon the product or service involved. If it essential to your health or work or family, it rises to a higher priority.

When it comes to the purchase of a car or house (or boat, plane, commercial property, RV, etc.), where the amount of money you are spending is significant, pay very close attention to the language of contracts. There are lots of documents associated with these types of transactions. Most of the documents' language is "boiler-plate," which simply means it has been drafted and structured by lawyers to be used in every transaction of that type, and not to be varied. As a result, terms are rarely negotiable.

Regarding negotiation, what is your position? Sometimes there are only two choices: you either accept the terms and conditions of purchase or use, or you don't. This applies to software, for instance. Opening the seal on a package constitutes agreement.

If you do have any negotiating leverage, such as asking to lower the price of a product or service in exchange for providing some-thing of value, or because something of value is lacking in the contract to justify the price, consider consulting an attorney. One of the best examples of this is buying a house, which is discussed below.

Also, how complicated is the agreement? How many pages is it? If it is short enough for you to review in a manager's office, including reading the fine print, don't worry about running it by an attorney (depending on the amount of money and importance of the contract).

Another consideration is quite personal. If you have trouble with focus or comprehension, or if you're not fluent in English, hire a lawyer, check with a paralegal, or schedule a call with an attorney at an online service like legalzoom.com.

Regarding attorney payments, seek a flat fee for a contract review. If, however, negotiation or rewriting the agreement is involved, these additional services would likely be charged on an hourly basis.

Kimberley Buol Ribordy, who specializes in real estate law in the greater Chicago metropolitan area, believes strongly in having an attorney review and/or facilitate your home ownership contract. Why leave the biggest investment of your life up to real estate agents and title companies that more often than not have no relationship with the consumer? Also, a real estate agent's fiduciary obligation is to the seller alone because the seller pays the commission.

When inspection issues arise, for instance, a real estate agent is not an advocate for the buyer's best interests. The agent wants to get the house SOLD. A real estate lawyer will make sure the consumer's interests are well represented, read everything in the contract and make recommendations or perform negotiations on the buyer's behalf, and perhaps most importantly, protect the consumer in the event of default.

Think about the stories in this book that involve home ownership. A lawyer would have prevented all those scenarios. So when you're considering the importance, price, and ability to negotiate a contract, factor in the expense, time, and stress of handling these disaster scam scenarios on your own. A stitch in time saves nine, even if that first stitch costs quite a lot.

Real estate law, by the way, is the least lucrative of all the law specialties. An attorney might handle your contract and closing for a flat fee of $750 to $1,000, depending on the market rate in your geographic and demographic area.

In summary, here are the general steps to follow in reviewing a contract:

- Examine the contract from a high-level, "deal term" standpoint. What are you agreeing to do (or not do)? Understand your rights and responsibilities under the agreement.

- What do you expect to get out of the agreement? Are your expectations being met?
- Make sure the agreement's business terms accurately reflect the deal (price, amount, duration, etc.)
- Fill in all the blanks and make sure the information is accurate.
- Calendar all important dates and/or deadlines to ensure you fulfill your responsibilities under the contract.
- Beware of automatic renewals, especially with online agreements.
- Are you being asked to hold the other party harmless from liability or to indemnify them? If so, carefully review this language and try to minimize its terms.
- Determine what's the worst that can happen to you if you "default" under the agreement. Can you meet your obligations? What triggers a default by the other party?
- What type of remedies do you need or expect from the other party if they default under the contract?
- What are the requirements for terminating the agreement, both for you and the other party?
- What happens if there's a dispute? Are you required to go to court to enforce your rights, or do you have the option to mediate or arbitrate the dispute, which could save you considerable time and money?
- Don't represent anything that's not true or say you will do something you can't or won't. Make any representations to the other party as narrow as possible.

- If other documents are referred to or "incorporated" into the agreement, know what they are and read those as well. They become part of the contract you're signing.
- Always try to identify ways you can limit your liability.

Bottom line: approach any agreement with the respect it deserves. You are making commitments through a contract. Make sure you know your rights and responsibilities under the agreement.

ENSURE AN **EFFECTIVE GUARANTEE**

One of the things I'm most proud of at TrustDALE is our Make It Right Guarantee. You see, most guarantees allow the company to remain in charge of the resolution process, which can and often does allow bias to creep in. Our guarantee offers the highest level of protection in the marketplace, because all of our companies have agreed, in writing, to relinquish control and place TrustDALE in full charge, not only of the resolution process, but of the outcome. In my experience, a company has to be pretty confident in its ability to deliver to put a third party in full control.

Any financially significant purchase should come with a guarantee; otherwise, what happens if a product breaks or a service simply stops showing up? We are, by now, familiar with the added and extended warranties and guarantees you can purchase on cars and technical equipment. Ask about, examine, and, of course, read guarantees to make sure they aren't just fluff and will prove effective when needed.

A guarantee may also be called a warranty, which is a type of

Any financially significant purchase should come with a guarantee; otherwise, what happens if a product breaks or a service simply stops showing up?

guarantee. By either name, it assures a consumer that the goods or services being purchased are worthy of the price, and that if something goes wrong, the company will stand behind their product. There are different types of warranties. An implied warranty is the promise under the Uniform Commercial Code that the goods purchased are what they say they are and there is nothing wrong with them. An express warranty is a promise made regarding the item or service sold. A full warranty means the consumer gets their money back, a replacement, or a repair. A limited warranty is limited by time and/or the action taken. By the way, the extended warranty offers people get in the mail for their cars are not warranties at all, but service contracts sold separately from the item.

Companies that offer extraordinary guarantees rarely have to make good on them. Often, people either don't know about the guarantee or are too busy to pursue the paperwork or even find the guarantee, which they should keep in a binder or folder of similar papers, or scan into their computer.

One man who read Tupperware's lifetime guarantee decided to test it out. Louie was determined to replace his mother's fifty-year-old Tupperware, which was cracked and deteriorating, as any similar product would be after five decades of wear and tear. Tupperware no longer had the exact same items, but was willing to give him credits toward purchasing new products at new prices, plus shipping and handling. That did not fly with Louie after he refreshed his memory by reading Tupperware's Full

Lifetime Warranty, although it does state the consumer will need to pay shipping and handling. He wanted to replace his mother's entire set at no cost.

All it took was a call from TrustDALE for Tupperware to back up its lifetime warranty in full, with no credits issued to apply toward a new purchase. A company with their reputation doesn't want to be embarrassed by quibbling over such a small matter. Their replacement guarantee was indeed effective, and the company is deserving of loyalty as far as TrustDALE and Louie (and his mom) are concerned.

When it comes to **ethical negotiation, equitable contracts**, and **effective guarantees**, what I am really talking about is trustworthiness. That is the basis of **ensuring your deal**. If you are interacting with an individual or company that does not operate from the core value of respecting and serving the consumer, you will not be able to ensure a good deal for yourself. Forget gimmicks and discounts; if your deal does not have the three elements we've discussed, you are in danger of falling victim to some variation of a Fast Funds Found fraud or being taken advantage of in the Rip-Off Range.

I'm a big believer in human contact when it comes to judging whether a company is **ethical**. Anyone can say all the right things on the phone, especially if they're reading from a script. I want to sit down and look the salesperson, manager, or owner in the eye and experience their whole body response to my questions. I want to know if they understand their product thoroughly and are proud to represent it.

Here are things to consider in a face-to-face interview with a salesperson, staff member, technical consultant, manager, supervisor, or owner:

- Does he or she show by words and actions that you are a valued customer?
- Is there more talking/selling than listening to your concerns?
- Does the person have an attitude of superiority or of helpfulness?
- Can you get all your questions answered without being redirected to peripheral issues or other products?
- Do you have enough time to read their contract in their office, line by line, or do you feel pressured to sign without reading it?
- If a guarantee is offered, who ensures follow-through of the guarantee? Get contact information ahead of when you need it.
- If a fair price has been negotiated, and then something not agreed upon is added or inserted at the very end of your conversation, you have to be able to get up and walk away. Something isn't right.

In the beginning of building TrustDALE's roster of companies, I was reluctant to endorse any oil change services because there are so many variables regarding what can go wrong. If someone's car develops a problem after an oil change, people tend to think something was broken or tampered with. After I talked to Phil Mendell, VP of Havoline Xpress Lube, however, I felt differently. He will get in touch with a consumer within minutes of receiving a complaint or concern and make a decision to do something special for them. It immediately defuses the situation, buying time to investigate what really happened and find a solution that satisfies everyone. Havoline has been one of TrustDALE's certified and guaranteed companies for eight years. They have managed to grow while still maintaining their principles of service. That demonstrates to me that they are ethical, equitable, and effective partners in the consumer/service-provider relationship.

About a year ago I crossed paths with the VP of Stanley Steemer, Bill Bradley. We talked about the philosophy of one of my favorite motivational speakers, Simon Sinek, author of *Start with Why*. We connected over admiration for one of Sinek's quotes from the book: "Our goal is to find customers that believe what we believe . . . in pursuit of the same goal." I am convinced that Stanley Steemer is a company with a value proposition similar to my own. The leader of a company sets the tone for all employees, who then pass on those values, which are delivered with professionalism, to the customer. In return, the customer values the company, demonstrated by return business and word-of-mouth recommendation. You might not get to meet the VP of Stanley Steemer or most companies you trade with. But you can look for cues to the company's value proposition. Do they know their product? Do they answer your questions, and are they eager to follow up after the sale? This is what happens when you have **ethical negotiation**, **equitable contracts**, and **effective guarantees**.

ENSURE YOUR DEAL

- ENSURE ETHICAL NEGOTIATION by asking as many questions as you can about qualifications, background, and history, including questions about the origins of any product involved (like a car). Verify the answers with evidence-based proof from the seller and your own research, and walk away from late surprises.

- **ENSURE AN EQUITABLE CONTRACT** by being certain your deal is a win for both you and the company; it cannot be equitable if it benefits only one side. Examine the language of the contract for fine print or clauses that will be to your disadvantage should issues arise.

- **ENSURE AN EFFECTIVE GUARANTEE** by asking for one if it is not offered; sometimes it costs extra to purchase, but it may be worth it if it includes money back for unsatisfactory performance or repair/replacement if something breaks. Store papers safely and know whom to contact in case you have to follow up.

CHAPTER 5

AUTHENTICATE YOUR DEAL

D E A L

DALE'S CASE STUDY FILES
Hiring a Stranger: Marjorie

At eighty-three years old, Marjorie was independent enough to live on her own. She could not, however, clean her gutters herself. When a man knocked on her door and offered to clean her blocked gutters for just $50, it sounded like a bargain. He represented himself as a handyman who had done work in the neighborhood.

The man said he would have to go to the hardware store to get some things first, which she understood. She wrote him a small check for supplies. He returned, did the job, Marjorie paid him, and he left. Two weeks later a man and a woman wearing Home Depot aprons knocked on her door and presented her with a $183,000 bill for the line of credit the "handyman" had opened in her name.

"I know how awkward this is, and we can imagine how embarrassing this would be if the police showed up to investigate this unpaid bill. We prefer to deal with these things quietly," the man said. "If you'll just get your pocketbook, we'll follow you to your bank and you can settle this here and now, no questions asked." Marjorie, scared out of her wits, complied, withdrawing $183,000 to give these uncredentialed clowns in stolen Home Depot aprons.

When she had calmed down enough to think clearly, she called her daughter, who called the police and found out a half dozen people had been scammed in the same way. People called in to identify these unprincipled crooks from a surveillance video. Their identities were confirmed, but the cash had already been spent on drugs and no money was ever recovered.

It's true that perhaps Marjorie shouldn't have been living alone if she was so easily bamboozled. At the least, she needed a "trust partner"—a relative, friend, or neighbor; maybe even a social ser-vices representative—to double-check on the situation before driv-ing to the bank and withdrawing that amount of money. Many of us have elderly relatives or friends who would have easily been taken in by a stranger offering to clean the gutters for $50.

Seniors are one of the most lucrative demographics for scammers to target. This is why consumers must have a plan in place for their loved ones who are older or cognitively disabled. Don't wait until something happens. Act now!

This dear lady jumped on what she thought was both a bargain and a blessing. Instead of having to shop around for services and compare value, someone just showed up at her door. She was too trusting. That is not the world we live in today.

If someone you don't know knocks on your door and offers to do a job for a very low rate, JUST SAY NO. It's not worth the risk.

Even for what seems like a straightforward job, like cleaning the gutters—which families used to manage for themselves, and if they couldn't, a neighbor might be willing to do so—consumers MUST see some kind of credentials. You can't take a chance on someone who is not bonded and insured falling off a ladder on your property. You don't know the true motives of the person at your door.

Questions must be asked and answered. Marjorie may have asked what experience the stranger at the door had, but she did not check up on it. When he claimed to have cleaned gutters for others in the neighborhood, she did not take names and make calls. Did she know what equipment he went to buy and ask for a receipt? No. She failed to **authenticate** anything about the stranger. I certainly hope her loved ones or community members supported her in making better decisions after that unfortunate incident. She was manipulated into parting with a big chunk of her savings.

Simon Sinek, mentioned in chapter 4, says in his book *Start with Why* that there are only two ways to influence behavior: manipulation or inspiration. Advertising and marketing professionals know all about manipulation. It works because humans are highly susceptible to suggestion.

Whether manipulation is negative depends a lot on who is doing the manipulation and why. An individual or company out to take advantage of consumers will use every trick and scam in this book, and more, to manipulate a consumer to participate in a bad, or lose-win, deal.

It is your perfect right to verify, validate, confirm, and corroborate any and all information from a seller. It is, in fact, your responsibility

It is your perfect right to verify, validate, confirm, and corroborate any and all information from a seller.

to **authenticate** the claims of an individual or company. Keep in mind *Caveat emptor!* Consumers are the ones left holding the bag and paying the bills when a good deal turns bad.

Assume your savvy consumer Cloak of Confidence. The information you absorb in this book allows you to say to yourself, or anyone, with poise and aplomb, "I wasn't born yesterday," "This isn't my first rodeo," "I've been to a bullfight, and I know how it ends," and the classic "If it sounds too good to be true, it probably is." YOU WILL NOT BE TAKEN FOR A FOOL.

Don't take anything for granted. It is easier than ever to **authenticate** claims via **references**, **reviews**, and **reports**. So let's get to it.

AUTHENTICATE **REFERENCES**

Ask a friend to describe what it means to get a "reference." Chances are, they'll tell you it's the act of asking for three current or former customers to vouch for a company that hopes to sell you a product or service. The fact is, getting a reference is one of the most overlooked and misunderstood steps in authenticating a deal. Let's start by identifying the most common types of references.

There are celebrity references (endorsements), friend references (referrals), client references a business has on file to validate the quality of their services, group references (an organization, like your church, might recommend a product or service owned by a church member), paid references that determine and rank businesses or individuals, and the blank blanket reference (as in "I have done work for your neighbors," but with no specifics).

A **celebrity reference** can lend credibility to a product or service for a nationwide audience. In addition, it draws attention to the brand name for top-of-mind recognition and can connect with consumers on an emotional level, linking feelings with a face we have seen in our living rooms and bedrooms, in movie theaters and magazines. This is true even though we know the celebrities are paid millions of dollars to recommend these brands—which absolutely negates the authenticity of the endorsement. Yet celebrity endorsements work.

References from friends and neighbors have a similar effect locally. Whether recommended by a friend, a friend of a friend, or someone in the community with a high standing or media visibility, consumers tend to believe claims of superior quality and service for the same reason they believe celebrity endorsements: credibility, top-of-mind recognition, and/or an emotional connection.

Trustworthy businesses know a **reference from a client** to a friend works like a charm. McKinsey, an international marketing and sales company, reported ten years ago that word of mouth is the primary factor behind 20 to 50 percent of all purchasing decisions, depending on the product. McKinsey also pointed out that when you start a sales call with a mention of a referral from a name the prospective customer recognizes, there is a higher level of trust from the beginning.

Nielson polls show that 84 percent of consumers say they either completely or somewhat trust recommendations from family, colleagues, and friends; consumers are four times more likely to buy something when referred by a friend.

Because references are so key to increasing business, if a company has no satisfied client comments (also known as testimonials) to give you, strongly consider

Because references are so key to increasing business, if a company has no satisfied client comments (also known as testimonials) to give you, strongly consider giving that enterprise a pass.

giving that enterprise a pass. It may not be a professional opera-tion. It doesn't matter if they are new; if you ask for references, a business should be able to produce them. It does matter, however, if those references are over a year old. You want references from the last few months or year—depending on the value of the prod-uct and time frame in which it is needed—as staff and quality of product may have changed in twelve to twenty-four months.

So ask for references, and more than one. Ask for twenty if you are making a big investment with a company. Any company, even one with bad reviews and a bankruptcy, may be able to come up with three references from the owner's or staff's friends and family. Twenty references show a company is not just relying on stand-ins for real customers, and you get to choose which three or four to contact.

If you're considering doing business with a friend you know from church or some organization you belong to, do yourself a favor and ask for references. Relationships have certainly been scuppered by doing business on a handshake and verbal promises, but worse, money has disappeared and projects have gone unfinished.

I have quite a cautionary tale about a **group reference** involving a church supposedly pushing a pyramid scheme for their members, none of whom asked for the references of the woman running the show. People were reassured when they saw a church was hosting the event—even though the church wasn't endorsing the event; they were just renting out the space.

This caper was called Friends Helping Friends (FHF), which offered to turn a $2,000 "gift" into $16,000. That opportunity drew 1,500 people to Power House of Deliverance Church in Greensboro, North Carolina, with hundreds to a thousand people at every meeting. Scamming people in groups oriented toward faith and positive thinking—and a need for a cash windfall—is a perfect business model for pyramid schemes.

The meetings attracted the interest of law enforcement due to the number of attendees. When police got involved, they realized FHF was a pyramid scheme. You pay money forward, but whether it comes back to you is debatable. The problem with pyramid schemes is that at some point, recruitment of new members stalls, so there is no more money coming in to distribute. This kind of program is unsustainable, and often illegal.

The problem with pyramid schemes is that at some point, recruitment of new members stalls, so there is no more money coming in to distribute.

The leaders of the meetings were told by police that pyramid schemes were illegal in that state, but they responded that this was simply a group of friends sharing financial love gifts to help one another. The penalty for violating the law against pyramid schemes was quite light at the time, so there wasn't a lot of motivation to "get out of town." It was a misdemeanor. Plus, consumers of these schemes don't want law enforcement to shut down their opportunity to make money—until they've lost their money and ask why it was allowed to happen.

Likewise, you should be wary of **paid references** that are veiled as good neighbor- or friend-based referrals. Companies often offer a finder's fee for homeowners to recommend companies to neighbors or friends. This doesn't necessarily invalidate the information, but you should ask your friend if they're being compensated for the referral. You should also look out for customer surveys that rank a prospective service provider on friendliness, competence, and so forth. Consumers are often paid for filling out these forms, so again, be sure to ask if the respondent was compensated in any way. An honest company should answer truthfully.

The **blank blanket reference** is another form of worthless referral. Remember what the stranger at the door gave Marjorie: "I've been doing work in your neighborhood for the last week," he said, gesturing to the houses lining the streets. These guys provide no evidence of references, but get by on showmanship.

The number-one problem with references, once they have been offered, is PEOPLE DON'T CHECK UP ON THEM. Prospective consumers by and large don't call, text, email, or have a face-to-face discussion with the person who is supposedly a satisfied customer. Why?

- They think they'll get to it later, and forget.
- They think if so-and-so is recommending a certain company, then it must be good and they don't have to ask (credibility).
- They remind themselves they've been meaning to get together with so-and-so and will make plans to do so, but they don't want to set it up immediately.
- They think of how nice it was to get together with so-and-so a year ago, but they do not call or text that phone number because they don't want to "bother" anyone (emotional connection).

A former DeKalb County, Georgia, school superintendent committed one of the most gigantic blunders regarding not checking references. He hired a search firm to go over online applications, the results of a nationwide search for a new human resources director. However, the superintendent already knew whom he wanted to hire: someone he had met at a cocktail party before the position was open. He talked the search firm into supporting his candidate as the best, and therefore the company, which was paid almost $39,000, did not authenticate the chosen job candidate's references.

That is how one of the largest school systems in the state ended up hiring a five-time convicted felon for six figures. This out-standing choice was supposedly an accomplished professional with an MBA and twenty years of experience. His résumé said he had directed HR departments at a pharmaceutical company and a security and transportation company. It did not mention that he had a criminal history that included burglary, theft, receiving stolen property, forgery, and violation of parole. This cocky con man was so sure no one would question his references that he signed a notarized statement saying he had never been convicted of violating the law. He also consented to fingerprinting.

That was the end of the road. You can fake your résumé and ref-erences, but not your fingerprints. Let's hope no school system is that careless in the future.

Friends, Romans, and countrymen: **authenticate your references!**

AUTHENTICATE **REVIEWS**

The most common method people use to **authenticate their deal** is to go to the court of consumer opinion: the internet. Why? It's super convenient and it's private. You know the drill. Many people check Yelp (yelp.com) regularly for reviews of everything. Angie's List (angieslist.com) originated as a paid subscription site, but now offers a level of free information where only mem-bers and verified third parties who have used the companies listed can post **reviews**. Consumers' Checkbook (checkbook.org), a project of the Center for the Study of Services, an independent nonprofit consumer advocacy group, is also a paid membership site, with local reviews for high-population areas of the country. Here's the problem: it's estimated that at least 15 percent of all online reviews are fake. The percentage is considered to be even higher for Amazon, Yelp, and eBay, yet that doesn't stop consumers from following them. Why? They're easy to find and require little effort. But here's what you need to consider: it's easy for companies to buy fake reviews. A consumer named Annie told me a story of a technician who arrived at her home and immediately offered her a discount if she'd go online and post a favorable review—before he'd opened his toolbox! Annie couldn't resist the 10 percent discount, but lived to regret it. She told me the work was so substandard it was practically worthless, but she realized

> *Here's the problem: it's estimated that at least 15 percent of all online reviews are fake.*

she'd destroyed any recourse she might have had due to her premature and glowing review. Humans tend to believe what they read. There's no more powerful example than to recall the mistake financial service companies Moody's and rival Standard and Poor's made by issuing AAA (the highest possible) credit ratings to risky pools of loans called collateralized debt obligations, or CDOs, prior to the great recession in 2007. Moody's admitted its mistake years later, but that didn't help thousands of investors who relied on those printed ratings (a form of review) and lost their shirts.

Here's a better way to look for and judge reviews. Put the name of the company into your web browser and add the word "reviews" or "complaints." Almost any business will have complaints, as you know if you look up your favorite restaurant and see it doesn't satisfy everyone. What you are looking for is a pattern of complaints about customer service, pricing, or quality of work. Pay less attention to complaints and atta-boys that lack specificity.

These days, companies can buy positive and negative reviews for about five dollars per post.

Tardiness and delays, rudeness over the phone or in person, smoking on your property, or leaving a mess behind may be due to a new or problematic employee and may not actually represent the company as a whole. But when you take all of these together, it speaks to a lack of accountability for customer service.

What you are looking for is a pattern of complaints about customer service, pricing, or quality of work. Pay less attention to complaints and atta-boys that lack specificity.

Next, go to the Better Business Bureau website (bbb.org). The BBB is a private nonprofit agency that helps people find and recommend, or censure, businesses, brands, and charities. Much like TrustDALE, the BBB's mission is to advance marketplace trust by setting standards, supporting best practices, promoting marketplace role models, calling out substandard marketplace practices, and creating a community of trustworthy businesses and charities.

The BBB assigns a business a grade of A, B, C, D, or F. This is based on a rating scale that includes time in business; volume of complaints (which are listed), including failure to answer or resolve complaints; failure to honor mediation/arbitration; transparent business practices; competency licensing; government action; and a few other categories.

Being mindful of the limitations of online reviews is important and should never replace the need for acquiring true, bona fide references when making an important buying decision.

AUTHENTICATE **REPORTS**

One thing government offices never get tired of is issuing **reports** based on formal complaints. Private citizens can and should access government websites such as www.usa.gov/state-consumer to check for complaints about a business. Although information varies by state, you can usually find a list of city, county, regional, and state consumer offices. These offices mediate complaints, conduct investigations, prosecute offenders of consumer laws, license and regulate professional service providers, provide educational materials, and advocate for consumer rights.

Contacts will be different in different states. In Illinois, for example, you would contact the attorney general's office in one of three areas of the state. Florida has a Department of Agriculture and Consumer Services, as well as a Seniors and Crimes website through the AG's office.

I once disqualified a pest control company from joining TrustDALE when I discovered it had been fined for using banned pest-control chemicals in consumers' homes. I wouldn't have known that had I not looked for the government-required disclosure of that fine on the Department of Agriculture's website.

The Federal Trade Commission's Bureau of Consumer Protection's mission is to stop unfair, deceptive, and fraudulent business practices. It collects complaints, conducts investigations, sues companies and people that break the law, and educates consumers and businesses about their rights and responsibilities. Go here to read more about the FTC/BCP: www.ftc.gov/about-ftc/bureaus-offices/bureau-consumer-protection. It is important to note the FTC only investigates and regulates companies that do business across state lines.

How businesses treat their employees is a good indication of how they will treat consumers. For instance, would you want to take your car to a car wash and oil change business that refused to pay a nineteen-year-old working a summer job in order to go to college?

How businesses treat their employees is a good indication of how they will treat consumers.

The US Department of Labor's Wage and Hour Division (WHD) is responsible for administering and enforcing some of the nation's most important worker protection laws. WHD is committed to ensuring that workers in this country are paid properly and for all the hours they work. You can check complaints at this office as well as file your own at www.dol.gov/whd/howtofilecomplaint.htm.

College student Tyler was smart enough to file a complaint with the Department of Labor after his employer at the car wash engaged in unlawful practices by not paying him. He never actually worked a full 11–6 shift, because if it wasn't busy, the owner required employees to clock out but not leave the premises in case business picked up. This is illegal. In addition, the owner withheld Tyler's last two checks, although he told me in a TrustDALE TV investigation that Tyler had cashed the checks. In all, he owed Tyler $800. This turned out to be one of my most memorable badguy ambush interviews. The car wash owner was stunned to see he was being held accountable for something he thought he'd long gotten away with. As I peppered him with questions about how he could do such a thing, he finally told me I could leave his property "in red lights or blue lights," meaning he would call the police or beat me up! It was okay; I'd gotten what I came for, and Tyler was about to get his.

It took a year for the Department of Labor to acknowledge receipt of Tyler's complaint, and another year to decide Tyler didn't have a case that was appropriate for them to litigate. However, he did get the green light for a civil suit in magistrate court, where his employer was ordered to pay him for his labor and was slapped with a fine for unlawful business practices.

> You might only find something on a business one out of nine times, but it is worth the research if the financial transaction is significant to you.

Sometimes government offices and courts do work for consumers, even if slowly. You might only find something on a business one out of nine times, but it is worth the research if the financial transaction is significant to you. **Authenticate** the quality of a company's product or service before you have a reason to take people to court.

This is where I make a shameless plug for TrustDALE. We do the **authenticating** for you. When we consider signing up a company, we want to be sure we are recommending and featuring a business that is impeccable and among the best at what they do. Client references are required, submitted, and CHECKED. We read reviews to get a sense of the public perception of our businesses. If there is a pattern of problems or cause for mistrust, that business will not be chosen as a TrustDALE partner. My staff checks the government sites and reports. At TrustDALE, we back our business partners with our $10,000 Make It Right Guarantee. If we miss something important in the process of authenticating a business's level of quality and customer satisfaction, I may end up having to pay a dissatisfied consumer $10,000.

AUTHENTICATE YOUR DEAL

- **AUTHENTICATE REFERENCES** by getting up to twenty references from a business and verifying your choices at once by phone, text, email, or in person.
- Authenticate a business's claims by **CHECKING REVIEWS** in the court of consumer opinion and on the Better Business Bureau website. Look for a pattern of taking advantage of consumers, not just complaints.
- **AUTHENTICATE GOVERNMENT REPORTS** that indicate formal complaints or lawsuits have been filed.

CHAPTER 6

LEGITIMIZE YOUR DEAL

D E A L

DALE'S CASE STUDY FILES

Tiny House, Big Problems: Julie and Boyd

Julie and Boyd looked forward to their retirement. They had a piece of land in Granbury, Texas, on which they planned to build a "tiny house."

The tiny-house trend is all about keeping things simple. Less square footage means fewer chores and maintenance. They are ecologically conscious since they have decreased environmental impact due to a reduced carbon footprint with less electricity and fuel output, plus fewer building materials (which are often recycled). Owners pay lower taxes, and quite possibly have no mortgage, which gives them a higher degree of self-sufficiency. It's a great idea.

The couple was excited when they wired over $22,000 in February 2017 for a high-performance, affordable, and "green" tiny-house kit. They had chosen to go with Dave Rades, owner of Kokoon

Homes in Toccoa, Georgia, who seemed to have a presence in the tiny-house segment of building.

What happened next didn't make Julie and Boyd's lives simpler or save them money. Instead, they spent a year and a half chasing down a builder who not only didn't deliver the tiny-house kit they paid for, but kept them tied up in court.

On the day of delivery, Julie and Boyd had assembled equipment and labor to help them get their dream home built. Only, the home didn't show up. Nor did it ever materialize. Rades had one excuse after another about why, and he refused to honor the couple's request to refund their money. In fact, there was no evidence had Rades ever delivered a home to anyone. Rades was a con man operating in the Rip-Off Range of deals between $500 and $50,000. He was a dream crusher.

I ran into Julie at a home show in Atlanta where Rades was scheduled to have a display. He didn't show up, but I couldn't help but notice she was wearing a T-shirt that said, "No Home, No Refund, No Kokoon," standing near his empty booth. Once I heard what had happened, the TrustDALE team mobilized to help Julie and Boyd in their quest for justice.

What we discovered is how hard it is for a wronged consumer to navigate law enforcement agencies and the court system without substantial support. Julie and Boyd believed taking payment for a house that was never delivered is theft. But it is very difficult to pursue a charge of criminal theft. The Stephens County Sheriff's Department turned Julie and Boyd away because their situation was seen as a civil, not criminal, case. The Toccoa Police Department also dismissed the issue. When the amounts are less than $50,000, local authorities often bow out, treating these cases as business disputes between individuals.

The couple tried to pursue a civil suit, but the two were worn down by delays that cost them more money. They dropped out when it looked like they would never be able to get a judgment in their favor.

It was apparent to TrustDALE that Dave Rades knew how to play the courts and law enforcement departments. Only a professional scammer who operated in the Rip-Off Range would know, for instance, that it would be excruciating to get a court or police department in small-town Georgia to take on an issue of theft that could be considered out of their jurisdiction. A key stumbling block was that Rades' business office was in Georgia, but his bank, where the money had been wired, was over the state line in North Carolina. Rades knew exactly what he was doing by having Julie and Boyd wire money to a different state, which would make him less accountable.

TrustDALE went to the Stephens County district attorney and convinced him to lean on the Toccoa Police Department to subpoena Rades' bank and office records. Eventually, Rades was charged with one count of felony theft by conversion and one count of conversion of payments for real property. In other words, the tiny house was not considered the stolen property, since the money for it was given willingly; it was the money that was considered the stolen property.

In the end, after more delays, the Toccoa Police Department issued a warrant for Dave Rades' arrest. He was sentenced to ten years in prison unless he repaid Julie and Boyd with scheduled installments of what he owed them. If he missed a payment, he would go to prison.

The best news is that Julie and Boyd invested in a tiny home with another company, out of Colorado, that delivered their product three weeks early. They now have exactly the kind of home they wanted—and they forced David Rades to give their money back. To keep up with this case, visit TrustDALE.com/media/on-demand/series/this-could-happen-to-you?id=xzdJM9qpG0g.

Learn from Julie and Boyd's mistake and never wire money to someone you don't know. Never wire money to a different state or country, since you will then be out of your own jurisdiction, with different laws applied to your financial interactions. Never wire all the money before you have received delivery of a product or service.

As an investigative reporter for both TV news stations and my TrustDALE Investigates video series, I have seen so many good people take these cases to court with high hopes, only to have them dashed on the rocky shores of a state court system's quirks. What seems cut and dried to consumers who have been scammed can turn into mush when they try to prove their case against a con artist who is skillful in navigating the game of no refunds.

An added complication is that magistrate court judges are not necessarily lawyers. They could be elected locals who lack the specialized knowledge your case requires.

> *TIP: When it is time to vote for judges, do it on the basis of legal merits rather than popularity, because you never know when or where you may be in court.*

Also, as Julie and Boyd found out, small-town police departments and county sheriffs don't want to get involved with disputes between individuals. For one thing, they rarely have the resources to deal with what might be considered civil disputes when they are pursuing criminal drug cases, which plague small towns across the country.

This is why it is so important for consumers to check into the legitimacy of a company or individual with whom they are doing business before entering into a legal agreement. Is the company licensed? Do they have liability insurance for their workers? Has the company been involved in prior lawsuits? If the company is going to send a person to your home and/or be in you or your loved one's personal space, have they been background-checked?

Is the company licensed? Do they have liability insurance for their workers? Has the company been involved in prior lawsuits? If the company is going to send a person to your home and/or be in you or your loved one's personal space, have they been background-checked?

Let me explain further what could happen if you skip any part of this step. A number of years ago, the California Supreme Court heard the appeal of *Fernandez v. Lawson.* Mr. Fernandez, a worker for Anthony's Tree Service, was injured while trimming a fifty-foot palm tree at the residence of Mr. Lawson.

Because California requires a contractor's license for trimming trees taller than fifteen feet, Lawson quite rightly requested proof of licensing from the owner of the tree service. He was shown a business card with the license number. He also asked if the company had workers' compensation insurance, but noticed the form he was given showed the insurance had expired. Excellent catch! The owner told Lawson he would bring current proof the next day. When the owner forgot the form the next day, however, Lawson gave in and allowed work to begin. Bad move.

Fernandez was injured—and the business was not insured. Moreover, the license number on the business card was an expired business license that had nothing to do with the work under contract.

Fernandez sued Lawson, claiming that because the tree service was in fact unlicensed, that made Lawson the employer, not the tree service, and thus he was required to have workers' compensation insurance. As if that wasn't bad enough, Fernandez contended that Lawson had violated the labor code by hiring an unlicensed contractor, violated California's OSHA (Occupational Safety and Health Act) provisions, and violated the American National Standards Institute's safety requirements for trimming trees.

Remember, this is all despite Lawson's attempts to validate that Anthony's Tree Service was licensed and insured, and reassurances that it was, which were lies.

The lower court initially ruled in favor of Lawson, holding that OSHA did not apply to noncommercial tree trimming at a private residence, which seems reasonable. The court of appeals reversed that judgment, holding that a person who hires an unlicensed contractor for work requiring a license is the employer of not only the unlicensed contractor, but any employees of that company. The court of appeals then ordered a new trial to determine if the owner of Anthony's Tree Service had intentionally defrauded the homeowner, and whether Fernandez had knowledge of that intent.

In the end, a state supreme court judge ruled that Lawson was not liable for the injuries, as a homeowner hiring a tree service for a domestic task could not be expected to know about compliance with OSHA's complex regulations system.

Any one of us could probably have leapt to that conclusion without spending all that time tied up in a mean-spirited court case, and spending thousands of dollars on lawyers' fees. Lawson had good instincts in checking on licensing and liability insurance for the tree service. But his desire to trust what he was told outweighed his personal obligation to require evidence of insurance. As for licensing, he was intentionally misled. Sadly, his deal to pay $450 for tree trimming turned into a lesson on getting ripped off.

LEGITIMIZE BY CHECKING **LICENSING**

How do you prove a company you are considering hiring is a real business? First of all, does it have a permit issued by a government agency allowing and authorizing it to conduct business within the government's jurisdiction—a business license? Ask the person you are doing business with if their company is licensed, if it operates as an LLC (limited liability company) or as a corporation, and what name is registered with the government (because sometimes it's under the owner's name, or the name of a past business, or something completely different).

But don't just take their word for it. You can find out if they are truly licensed by contacting the city or county clerk where the company is headquartered. Businesses are required to register with the state and to renew annually. The easiest thing is to search "secretary of state," add the name of the state where the company claims to be headquartered, and follow the prompts under "find a business."

Professional licenses that permit an individual to practice a specific trade or profession can be a factor as well. For instance, these professions need a professional license as well as a business license: cosmetology, medicine, nursing, architecture, HVAC contracting, electrical, and engineering. One of the first things I do when I visit a new doctor is look on their office wall for their MD. But if I were having a special procedure or surgery performed, I would also search the internet, before or after my appointment, to verify the doctor's professional accreditation.

It's not unusual for our team at TrustDALE to receive an email from a consumer telling us they have found a plumber, electrician, or heating and air technician who quoted a price that was half of what the certified professionals on my site offer. Early on in my business, I did quite a bit of research into these "professionals," only to learn they were not professionals, but unlicensed handymen who would get the work by charging a lower price. How could they afford it? They cut corners.

Consumers are highly susceptible to offers that are too good to be true. Now when I get one of these emails, I ask the consumer to give me the name and address of his preferred technician and a copy of his quote. To date, I have never found a single one of these technicians who could pass the investigative standard I use in my TrustDALE certification process, which requires professional licensing and liability insurance in fields where there is risk to property and health.

Just because the person claims to be licensed doesn't mean he is.

Just because the person claims to be licensed doesn't mean he is. I once busted a fake doctor who had made his way onto the staff of the University of North Carolina Medical Center. Most states' secretary of state offices maintain credentials for professionals and are easily discovered through an online search. If you can't find the credentialing body of the person you're considering doing business with, simply search the internet using the name of the profession and add the words "licensing body," or type "who licenses _____ in (my state)."

Some businesses require additional licenses, like a liquor store, or the food and beverage industry, which requires that certain staff members are licensed in food service safety.

As of February 2019, the state of Texas is considering removing licensing for cosmetologists, which includes hair stylists in salons. Currently, cosmetologists attend beauty school and go through 1,500 hours of training on average. Consumers who rely on salons for manicures and pedicures, and haircuts and hair color, may have a rude surprise if licensing is suspended. Beauty school teaches aspiring professionals how to safely handle chemicals. Improper usage could and has caused hair loss. Likewise, failure to sanitize footbaths and manicure tools could lead and has led to serious infections. In 2018, a man in Indiana had his leg amputated as a result of an infection he contracted from a pedicure.

This legislation was introduced to expand employment opportunities and remove unnecessary obstacles. But labeling cosmetology as a field in which the consumer "can be trusted to seek out the best service provider without any serious risk of harm" (as quoted by Matt Shaheen, the state representative who introduced the bill) is not at all accurate.

If you have trouble finding evidence that a business is licensed, that's a red flag signaling that you either need more information to verify the license, or you need to terminate your relationship with this business because it is not legitimate. Remember what happened to Lawson. Even though he attempted to legitimize the tree company's licensing, he did not follow through when time made it inconvenient to do so. Spare yourself the headaches!

LEGITIMIZE BY CHECKING LIABILITY INSURANCE

Make sure the company you are considering doing business with is insured, especially when it comes to contractors or anyone who will be in your home or on your property. This includes home-based businesses, no matter how small. Insurance, of course, is an added expense for a company that is reflected in the price for whatever service they offer. But accidents happen, and there's no telling if or when an accident could cause bodily harm or property damage.

> TIP: Do not ever lend your own equipment to contracted service workers—not a ladder, an extension cord, a drill, or a hammer. If an accident should occur, the contractor could say your equipment was faulty and make you pay for any damages.

Again, don't just take someone's word that their business workers and equipment are insured to protect you from liability. Ask for proof, and find out exactly what is covered by their business policies. Saving a few bucks with an uninsured company isn't worth the risk of living through a liability nightmare should something go wrong.

Saving a few bucks with an uninsured company isn't worth the risk of living through a liability nightmare should something go wrong.

Mandatory business insurance varies by company type, size, and individual state regulations. Here are some things to keep in mind about the different types of business insurance:

- **GENERAL LIABILITY INSURANCE** covers damages if a company's employees or products or services cause bodily injury or property damage to a third party.
- **A BUSINESS OWNER'S POLICY** (BOP) covers a number of bases that will reassure the consumer: property insurance, business interruption insurance, vehicle insurance, and crime insurance. With this kind of coverage, if something happens to one aspect of

the business, it could keep operating and fulfill its obligations to the consumer without too much of a lag.

- **COMMERCIAL AUTO INSURANCE** covers a company's vehicles. Homeowners need to know that any worker's vehicle on their property is properly insured. It's all too easy to open your garage door and automatically back out, forgetting there is a truck behind your car in the driveway. And there's always the chance your car could get nicked by someone else's careless driving or parking.

- **WORKERS' COMPENSATION INSURANCE** is an essential element of an ethical workplace. All employers with at least one employee must carry coverage for work-related accidents, illnesses, and even death. Subcontractors, independent contractors, and their employees should be covered unless they are independent enterprises. Construction businesses are required to have workers' compensation insurance. It's a red flag if a company can't prove they provide workers' comp, or has tried to get out of paying workers' comp claims, although the merits of individual claims vary.

- **PROFESSIONAL LIABILITY INSURANCE** (or errors and omissions insurance, E&O) is necessary for lawyers, medical and health providers, accountants, consultants, notaries, real estate agents, hair salons, and technology providers, to name a few.

LEGITIMIZE BY DOING A
LAWSUIT/BACKGROUND CHECK

Lastly, consumers should research whether the company they hope to work with has been involved in any lawsuits. This is super easy. Just search the term "online court records" and include the county where the company is headquartered. Follow the prompts to "find a case," type the name of the company into the search box, and hit return.

What you're looking for is whether a company frequents the magistrate court as a defendant. Companies can also show up as plaintiffs bringing an action against another company or individual; for instance, if they haven't been paid for services rendered. But that isn't what we're concerned about. Look for the number of times a company has been sued, and if they have won or lost. My rule of thumb is to consider it problematic if a company has been sued and lost more than two times in two years. Most legitimate companies go to great lengths to avoid being sued.

Small to medium-size companies that get sued often and successfully should be avoided.

Repeat this process with your state court clerk's office and the superior court clerk's office, searching at least five years of history. Cases in state and superior courts are less likely to involve business-to-consumer transactions, but results will give you a feel of how the business performs in the marketplace. Small to medium-size companies that get sued often and successfully should be avoided.

If you are hiring a company that will send a person to your home or be in a personal space with you or your loved ones, make certain the company performs criminal background checks of their employees prior to and periodically after their hiring. Some companies, as you'll learn in chapter 8, might background "check," but they don't necessarily background "decline." It's your right to ask the company to share its standards for hiring people who have broken the law. It's also your right to ask for the full name of the person who is coming to or entering your home. I have personally discovered and stopped uncomfortable situations for myself and others by searching the state Department of Corrections' past and present inmate database before a scheduled visit. The higher the risk, the more you should know.

Bankruptcy records are just as helpful. One method crooks use effectively in the Rip-Off Range is to declare bankruptcy and immediately reopen under a new name. You should never fail to ask a company representative directly if his organization or its leadership has filed for bankruptcy in the past ten years. If the tech doesn't know, call his superior and work your way up to the owner. If they don't want to answer, or they act suspicious, bankruptcy filings are public record and can be accessed at the federal bankruptcy court where the company is headquartered.

If you happen to live in an area where your court records are not yet online, you should consider driving to the courthouse where the company you're considering doing business with is headquartered. What might appear to be an inconvenient visit to the clerk of court's office to search the company's lawsuit history the old-fashioned way might end up saving you thousands of dollars and weeks of avoidable misery.

LEGITIMIZE YOUR DEAL

- **LEGITIMIZE BUSINESS LICENSES** by checking with

the city, county clerk's office, or the state for a record of registration. Investigate professional and additional licenses online, and/or ask them to show you. Remember to check the details to make sure the name is the same and it is up to date.

- **LEGITIMIZE LIABILITY AND OTHER INSURANCE TYPES** by asking to see the certificate or paperwork and making sure the details are correct.

- **LEGITIMIZE A COMPANY'S REPUTATION REGARDING LAWSUITS** by doing an online search for court records, going back five years.

CHAPTER 7

I'VE BEEN SCAMMED! NOW WHAT?

DALE'S CASE STUDY FILES
Failure to Follow DEAL: Dale

Yes, that Dale. Me. I want you to know that although I have years of consumer investigations under my belt and am an expert on uncovering scams, even I can get ripped off if I fail to follow my own advice. Read and learn. I share this also because this financially painful episode renewed my confidence that my seven-step *FFF/DEAL* approach works—if you work it.

Five years after launching TrustDALE.com, my team and I discovered an enterprise that could complement the website. In a media environment that assumed print was dead or dying, it turned out one area of print was thriving—direct-mailed home-service guides. In a crowded and confusing marketing environment, these simple booklets are quite successful at helping homeowners find professional companies they can trust. The printed guide was very similar to the TrustDALE website. Home-service companies would be required to meet a standard of performance and would sign an agreement to honor the TrustDALE Make It Right Guarantee. In turn, they would receive a listing in our certified services guide that included a phone number printed in the guide so the business would know the customer came from TrustDALE's recommendation.

We launched our guidebook in Tampa, Florida, with a core of twenty-five service companies representing heating and air, roofing, electrical, landscaping, window replacement, and more. The vetted and certified participating companies paid a set fee for each unique call. This was a simple pay-for-performance business model.

One day a man named Jeff Taylor dropped by my Atlanta office. Jeff told me he was president and cofounder of a company based in Bradenton, Florida, called Dewayne Thomas Media. He explained that they specialized in creating glossy magazines for home-service companies all over the US. He wanted to know more about TrustDALE because he saw potential in helping me grow my model across the entire country.

Several weeks of discussions turned into a ten-page agreement, signed December 30, 2014. It authorized Dewayne Thomas Publishing (a division of Dewayne Thomas Media) to sell the TrustDALE program to eligible companies across the US. TrustDALE would have full control over the vetting process, and because Dewayne Thomas Publishing would bear the expense of selling the product and publishing the magazine, it would receive 80 percent of the gross revenue. This was a multimillion-dollar deal that I, of course, verified with my lawyer.

Taylor knew I intended to mail a spring edition of the services guide in Tampa in January of 2015. Almost as an aside, he asked me how much I paid my current publisher and distributor for that mailing. When I told him, he immediately responded he could beat their price by an impressive margin. He said since our national deal would generate millions of dollars, he would offer his services for the Tampa guide at a "significant discount."

Payment for the printing and distribution of 160,000 Tampa services guides was set out in a one-page work order and two-page contract. The sum of $62,511 was required in full by December 31, 2014. TrustDALE's publishing arm, Cardwell Media, made three payments: two by wire transfer and one by check to Dewayne Thomas Publishing Inc., and we beat the December 31 deadline by two days.

It became apparent by February 2015 that something was wrong. The number of calls coming in from the guide was half the expected response. Jeff said he would visit every mail center involved and talk to the postal managers. His news was not good. He found that the US postal service had lost half, eighty thousand, of the guides that were printed and mailed out. Oddly, he said he knew of this happening before.

This was an incredulous story.

I had a responsibility to my clients, who were not getting the value they expected based on past performance. I demanded Jeff be accountable for the loss of our product. He seemed distraught, as if he wanted to make this right, and signed a contract to print an additional ninety thousand books if he could not produce evidence of his claim that the postal service was responsible for the lost books.

The relationship between TrustDALE, Cardwell Media, and Jeff Taylor became increasingly strained as weeks went by and Taylor could not support his accusations against the postal service.

Fortunately, our ten-page contract that I thought would create huge returns was cancellable by either party with written notice. Done.

In April, Taylor sent an email stating he'd gone ahead and printed the additional books to meet the obligation he made in the new contract, but in a new twist he demanded that Cardwell Media pay an additional $14,763.79 to cover the cost of mailing the books. To enforce his request, he gave us the receipts he claimed he had received from the US Postal Service, documenting the delivery of the books from the publisher and the payment in full for their mailing. If payment was not received, Taylor threatened to have our glossy home-services magazine guides shredded and recycled.

I had no choice but to pay Taylor's "ransom." However, I was not going to pay it to him or his company. I would pay it directly to the post office—and get to the bottom of this.

Jeff did not count on the fact that due to my thirty years of investigative reporting, I knew how to get in touch with postal inspectors. Several months later, when the postal inspector reviewed the receipts Jeff had given me as proof of mailing, he determined they were forgeries. Jeff not only hadn't mailed all of the guides, but he had overcharged me for postage as well.

According to US Postal Inspector B. D. Kramer, the real receipts showed Taylor had only printed 98,000 of the promised 160,000 guides. Kramer's investigation report, dated September 8, 2015, concluded, "Mr. Cardwell was given false and misleading information from Mr. Taylor and DTM (Dewayne Thomas Media)."

I filed suit against Taylor and his company in Fulton County Superior Court. Taylor met fire with fire and had his attorney attempt to move the suit to federal court jurisdiction in the state of Florida. Even though this appeared to be a clear case of both mail and wire fraud, and theft by conversion and perjury, I eventually paused the lawsuit because—with all the delays and maneuverings—it would cost me more money to pursue than I could effectively collect.

Everyone makes mistakes, but it is painful to remind myself how I ignored my own best advice. This is one of the reasons I want to share my FFF/DEAL model with consumers. If you learn by my bad example, then I consider my temporary lapses of judgment a gift to you, which makes me feel better.

If I were to have properly vetted Taylor and his company, I would have found a record of petty crimes and judgments in Florida courts. If I had paid him with a credit card, I would have been able to dispute the charges when he failed to deliver the agreed-upon product. When I tried to hold him accountable in court, he misused the court system. But that wasn't the worst part.

Even though the US postal inspector concluded fraud had been committed, he declined to prosecute. Why? Remember the lessons of the Rip-Off Range: con artists know—but regular citizens don't know—that law enforcement have nondisclosed thresholds a crime must meet before they will prosecute. I'm told the federal court's threshold to prosecute postal fraud is a minimum of one million dollars.

There's nothing like a bucket of ice-cold water over your head to remind you to practice what you preach. As a parent, a bona fide investigative reporter, a successful businessman, and a high-functioning man with a message and a mission, I was an authority figure. But, like anyone, I can be distracted by flattery and thoughts of huge profits from a small investment. It was a good reminder I am human, just like you.

So, you've been scammed! Now what? You do what babies do when they are learning to walk. They fall, throw a fit, scream, whimper, take a deep breath . . . and get back on their feet.

WHAT YOU SHOULD KNOW
ABOUT THE COURT SYSTEM

Scammers depend on the fact most Americans don't understand and therefore are intimidated by our courts. It doesn't help that in my experience, the people who work in the court system—perhaps because of volume—do not make it consumer friendly. Even though I've warned you about the pitfalls of taking your case to the courts, if you have good cause to consider legal action, the more you know the less intimidating it is. Here is a breakdown of what courts do, with my observations and caveats.

The term "magistrate court" has replaced what used to be called small claims court. This court hears cases involving civil claims of $15,000 or less and allows ordinary citizens to represent themselves without hiring an attorney. The filing procedure is inexpensive, under $200. Forms and instructions are provided to assist individuals in their pursuit of justice.

Don't confuse magistrate court with *Judge Judy* or any of the other TV courtroom shows, which don't take place in real courtrooms and don't present real trials, although they may be real cases. Those shows feature arbitrations, a legal method for resolving disputes outside the court that is less formal in its rules and procedures. A neutral third-party arbitrator, in *Judge Judy's* case a real judge, hears the case, examines the evidence, and makes a binding decision within the parameters of arbitration—and the contract signed with the media company that produces the show.

What is similar to a courtroom drama is that the parties in magistrate court are adversarial, and they need hard copies of all the documentation relevant to their cases. This goes back to the first step of my DEAL formula: as you define what you need, document everything relevant to your purchase or agreement so you have a folder of receipts and written proof of conditions of delivery, quality, warranties, etc.

The most common problem a consumer faces in magistrate court is when the defendant doesn't show up. The court will usually give your adversary a second chance. A savvy company that has been taken to court before will often send an attorney to the second hearing to ask for a continuance, which is normally granted. The defendant's goal is to frustrate you with delays until you decide it's no longer worth your time or money.

The defendant's goal is to frustrate you with delays until you decide it's no longer worth your time or money.

Even if and when you win a judgment, you're just beginning the difficult process of collecting the debt. If a company has declared bankruptcy or has been dissolved, there may be no money to return.

Also, in most states, companies can appeal the judgment and take it to state court. That freezes the judgment until it can be scheduled in the higher court, where you will need to hire an attorney. Although an attorney is not required by law, courts and judges frown on people who file cases in a higher court without the aid of an attorney.

State court enforces the laws, rules, and regulations of a given state and applies and interprets that state's own constitution. The difference between state courts and federal courts is jurisdiction.

Cases that involve family disputes, dispossessions, misdemeanors, and traffic violations are heard by state courts.

Superior court is responsible for handling cases involving serious crimes (felonies), civil disputes, real estate matters, and family domestic relations issues.

Federal court is limited to issues related to the US Constitution and provided for by Congress. This is also the venue for bankruptcy proceedings and civil disputes between citizens of different states when the amount exceeds $75,000. Federal court is also the venue for about 80 percent of all class-action suits.

TrustDALE has helped many consumers pursue justice. A video camera, my big mouth, and persistence, as well as experience, can make a difference in unraveling the details of a bad deal and pressing for repayment or retribution. But we can't be everywhere and do everything for everybody. We have our limits. And that is why I'm relying on you, the consumer, to learn, practice, and know what you need to do to protect yourself, your family, and your property. Check our blog stories, informational articles, and video presentations at TrustDALE.com to help remind you what's at stake and to keep your skills sharp.

GET YOUR DOCUMENTS IN ORDER

This is the first step to any issue. Hopefully, you've documented your deal, saving receipts and keeping notes on key elements, like names of people you spoke with, dates of interactions, and any forms you signed, of course.

If you find you've done a poor job collecting records prior to discovering the fraud, it might not be too late. Going forward, document everything that may be pertinent. Take photographs and videos. Record phone calls. Fewer than a dozen states require two-party consent to record phone conversations: California, Connecticut, Florida, Illinois, Maryland, Massachusetts, Montana, New Hampshire, Pennsylvania, and Washington. That could change: for instance, Illinois found the two-party consent statute unconstitutional in 2014. Simply search online for the state where the person you hope to record is located and include the words "two-party consent to record phone conversation" to find out if it is legal.

> *If you find you've done a poor job collecting records prior to discovering the fraud, it might not be too late.*

Going forward, it is essential that you never lose your temper. I know this can be incredibly difficult, especially with con artists, but you gain nothing by showing your frustration and anger.

If, however, the other side loses its temper, you may be able to use some of what's said to you in private in the courtroom (which is why it's important to know whether the state requires two-party consent to recorded conversations). Go ahead and record your conversation if you're able to do so safely. Leave immediately if any physical threats are made, of course. Participating in an angry duel of words that turns into a power struggle will not help you. If these are bad guys, they could be dangerous.

DETERMINE INTENTION

Determine as soon as possible, whether the person or company that scammed you did it intentionally or due to an unforeseen circumstance. If it was intentional, there is usually a pattern, and an internet investigation will reveal other offenses. If it was unintentional, the company will have findable offices and will pick up their phones, as opposed to con artists who use fictitious names and contact info and don't register their businesses with the city, county, or state. Set up a person-to-person appointment to discuss what to do next.

Review the problem. Hopefully you have documentation that allows for a grievance procedure and warranty process. Be sure to submit in writing a detailed list of what went wrong, and what you expect to be done about it. You may be able to work out an acceptable compromise with a legitimate company that is having problems meeting its obligations. Reputable companies will work with you, but respectful dialogue can only take place when both sides maintain cool heads.

Here is how that worked with someone who accepted responsibility for his scam and was accountable for his actions (it does happen).

I got a phone call from a woman who said she had the strangest solicitation. It was a voicemail encouraging her to vote for a politician. The phone number corresponded to the offices of the Georgia state government. This was clearly improper, as state phones cannot be used to solicit campaign support, so I went to her home and recorded the message left on her phone.

The department of state services informed me that the phone number was assigned to State Representative George Maddox. State representatives get two free phone lines for their office, and can also have one or two lines installed in their homes for constituent services. They are for state business only, not personal usage.

When I called Representative Maddox and described the situation, he said without pause or embarrassment that it was his telemarketing business. He sold phone lines and automated voicemail setups to politicians and stores. He had twelve phone lines in his home that he used to solicit business. It worked well for him because he could undercut his competitors on price since he didn't have to pay for the phone lines.

He was surprisingly apologetic when I reminded him that tax-funded state phones could not be used for private business. It seemed he had not absorbed that information, which was probably in a binder of rules and regulations given to him when he was elected. It never occurred to him what he was doing was illegal and improper, and he wanted to make things right.

Not a single law enforcement authority lifted a finger to prosecute him. The problem went away, probably because he was honest about it—but perhaps also because the state couldn't explain why they had allowed so many phone lines to be installed in the first place with no follow-up on whether they were being used for state business.

THE SPECIAL CASE OF THE HOME-BUILDING INDUSTRY

The home-building industry is famous for robbing Peter to pay Paul. A builder uses funds paid in advance by one client to pay off the bills from his previous project. This is an unfortunate accepted practice that, through no fault of the builder, can spin out of control if there is a downturn in real estate. If a company has any hope of recovering and wants to stay in business, it will cooperate with your efforts to come up with a schedule and a payment plan. If this is the case, ask for a confirmable list of the builder's assets.

You'll want some kind of personal guarantee as well. Part of

America's greatness is that we don't have debtor courts, and people can start over by filing bankruptcy. But one of the most frustrating aspects of having a builder fail to deliver is that contractors can create a corporation or LLC and effectively put a firewall between their business and their personal assets. Many contractors are serial bankruptcy participants. They avoid the seven-year rule between bankruptcy filings by placing the business in the name of their spouse or other relatives. A personal guarantee penetrates that firewall, but here's a warning: most fraudulent contractors will be one step ahead and have their personal assets under someone else's name. Before you dive into a long and difficult court case, hire a company to do an asset search. You'd rather pay $200 to determine if someone has assets before you spend $10,000 to earn a judgment only to find the company is broke.

HARNESS THE POWER OF ONLINE REVIEWS

Well-intentioned companies are concerned about what consumers say about them. Business reviews and social posts can shape a company's image. I don't recommend firing off an angry email to Yelp or any other site before attempting a direct path of resolution with the company or individual. But if you have tried discussion and negotiation with no results, go ahead and add your assessment to the court of consumer opinion.

Most people under a certain age who believe they've been scammed will automatically alert their friends and family via phone, text, email, Facebook, Instagram, and Twitter, including photos or video if pertinent. That's a given. But while the grapevine is effective, it doesn't guarantee you'll reach a wide-enough audience to impact a company that wants to maintain its reputation, whether because it wants to keep scamming people or because it is genuinely concerned about its image.

Yelp, after all, averages 178 million unique visitors a month. Angie's List reaches 6 million households. Then there are other sites like ripoffreport.com. Search the company's name and add the word "complaint." That can lead to various websites and comments where you can connect with other people who may have been scammed by the same business. If they are further along in the process of collecting information or filing a criminal complaint or civil suit, you can compare notes. There's power in numbers.

Don't say any-thing that would embarrass you if you had to read it back to someone objective.

When writing your review, use appropriate language and don't embellish. Don't say anything that would embarrass you if you had to read it back to someone objective. As with your personal social media outreach, use photos or video to back up your grievance.

Many consumers consult the Better Business Bureau as an ultimate authority. The BBB takes your online complaints very seriously. As a veteran journalist, I've worked with the BBB in many states. People have differing opinions about the bureau, but I find it a good place to learn whom you should not do business with. A company that has a D or an F will likely show a pattern of negative feedback, or they don't answer the BBB's request to respond to complaints.

Sometimes companies don't understand how the BBB works. I consult with a company in Atlanta that once had Ds and Fs associated with most of their locations. My colleagues and I had secret-shopped many of those locations, however, and found their service to clearly be above average. This was a real mystery. A closer review found the locations with bad grades had only received one or two complaints over a multi-year period, but the company had never responded to the BBB's request for information as part of the resolution process. Within three months, every store location was upgraded to an A or a B.

MAKE A STINK

Reputable businesses dislike, and in fact are upset by, less than four stars on review sites caused in part by a complaint that won't go away. You can leverage this by offering to remove or update your complaint if the company agrees to meet your reasonable demands. After getting no satisfaction from calling local Sprint offices, a friend's son posted a complaint on social media about how Sprint had preyed upon his parents to load them down with extra charges for things they didn't need. All he had to do was to imply elder abuse (even though his over-sixty-five parents still have all their marbles) and corporate customer service was on the phone immediately to clear up the misunderstanding and request that he take down his complaint, which he did.

I once made a scene in the lobby of a hotel that claimed "your complete satisfaction or 100 percent of your money back!" My family had checked in late the night before only to learn the hotel was overbooked. The entire city was full and we had no choice but to take a one-bedroom instead of the two-bedroom suite we had reserved. To make matters worse, the room reeked of cigarettes. The next morning when I asked for a refund, I was told the manager was not on duty and they couldn't refund my money. I politely held up the laminated guarantee I'd found in the room and stated to a packed lobby that my family had been baited and switched on our rooms and the hotel was refusing to honor its guarantee.

Unfortunately, five minutes later I was escorted from the lobby by local police officers, even though my protest was, of course, nonviolent. Since I had registered the room on a credit card, when I returned home I initiated a dispute of the payment. After providing a written statement and my evidence, my card service refunded my money.

Remember the story in chapter 6 about the tiny house that was never delivered? Julie first caught our attention at a home show where she was wearing a T-shirt with the words "No Home, No Refund, No Kokoon," which was the name of the company that had stiffed them. Now the owner of that company has to pay them back or go to prison.

I was once able to get a van I bought repainted by the dealership by calling to let them know I was going to show up in two days wearing a sandwich board that read "XX Sells Peeling Vans." I won't mention their name here because they did agree to repaint the van.

If you do mount a protest, be prepared for pushback. The company may threaten you by claiming they'll file a lawsuit or call the police. Don't be intimidated, but be sure to stay off private property. You have a right to protest on the public right-of-way, which is generally the space measured from the side of the road and extending eight feet toward the business. This form of self-expression might seem outdated, but you'll be amazed at the results you can get with a sign bearing a creative (and truthful) message.

FILE A CRIMINAL COMPLAINT

If you aren't getting anywhere with the previous steps and feel you can prove fraud, consider filing a criminal complaint. Most law enforcement agencies will allow you to document your displeasure, but the solicitor or district attorney will rarely prosecute in the Rip-Off Range—what they consider business disputes to be settled between individuals.

TrustDALE has had great success overcoming this hurdle by documenting that the business has a pattern of similar behavior that gives grounds for charges to be filed. You can sometimes find fellow victims on social media, as we have discussed. If you don't immediately find others who have been treated the same way as you, post your situation and ask that it be shared to reach the widest audience possible to attract anyone else who has been defrauded. Ask fellow victims to file police reports in their jurisdictions, and then take those reports to your district attorney's office. While these professionals are overwhelmed with cases, most have white-collar crime divisions that will at least give your concern a hearing. Con artists who realize they're about to be arrested if they don't pay you back suddenly find great incentive in making it right.

SEEK A CRIMINAL
WARRANT WITHOUT POLICE AID

If you are having a hard time getting law enforcement to take an interest in your situation, I suggest you search the term "theft by deception and theft by conversion" and enter the name of your state along with the word "code." If it appears one or more of the tenets of the code fit your situation, you can apply for a criminal warrant in the criminal division of magistrate court in the county where the crime took place. Most people don't do this because 1) they don't know they can, and 2) law enforcement and the courts steer you toward the civil-court path.

If you choose to seek a warrant, make certain you have the evidence you need. You can hire an attorney to assist, but it is not necessary in order to file. The judge will consider your evidence and determine if a hearing is warranted. If so, he or she will issue a summons for the alleged offender/s to appear in court to defend themselves before issuing a warrant.

Be warned, it is often just as hard for law enforcement to locate the person summonsed for a criminal warrant as it is a civil warrant. If the judge decides to issue a warrant for arrest, you've cleared one hurdle. Now it is up to the solicitor or district attorney to determine whether there are grounds to prosecute. This might be the end of the road when it comes to having the person tried, but you might receive some measure of satisfaction by having the person booked, photographed, and publicly charged with an offense, which could serve as a warning to future victims.

FILE A CIVIL COMPLAINT

Let's be clear. Attempting to get someone arrested as described above might make you feel better, but a person in jail will have a hard time paying you back. If you'd rather focus on a refund, consider filing a civil complaint as a last resort. But be warned, I've seen so many people go down this path only to spend more money trying to collect than what was owed them, which is not a good deal. Con artists know how to play the legal system. If you are fortunate enough to win a judgment, your journey has only just begun. There are several more mountains to be climbed before you're likely see a penny. In this case, an ounce of prevention is worth tons of cure.

I would advise you to seek a consultation with an attorney before you pay an attorney or file a case on your own. Most will give you a straight answer about your chances of prevailing. You can't let your emotions drive your decision. Reputable companies don't want the black eye of losing a magistrate court judgment, but con artists couldn't care less and will risk court again and again.

FILE AN OFFICIAL REPORT

This is likely your final action, as in my experience it's the least likely to get you a result. But it will serve as a warning to others. Years ago, the Federal Trade Commission was a feared entity, able to assess multimillion-dollar fines against companies that defrauded people across state lines. While the FTC continues to pursue judgments and settlements, years of budget cuts have reduced it to little more than a warning platform. Even so, I include the FTC and the Governor's Office of Consumer Protection (or state agencies by similar names) in my proactive DEAL checklist, as well as platforms you should engage after the fact. Why? Because I believe it is your civic duty to warn others and help them avoid a similar fate.

Public board orders are hard to have removed, and you can use them to plant red flags for your fellow consumers. If your scammer has or was supposed to have a professional license, report their activity to your secretary of state. If your contractor holds a certification with a nongovernmental trade group, ask that trade group to intervene or terminate his credentials. At the end of the day, reputable businesses don't want this stain on their records.

I'VE BEEN SCAMMED! NOW WHAT?

If you've fallen victim to a scam, follow these steps to seek restitution:

- **UNDERSTAND THE DIFFERENT LEVELS OF THE COURT SYSTEM** and how they apply to your situation.
- **GET DOCUMENTS IN ORDER** and continue to document interactions.
- **DETERMINE THE OFFENDER'S INTENTION** regarding their scam.
- **HARNESS THE POWER OF ONLINE REVIEWS** if the company refuses to negotiate. Alternatively, you can **MAKE A STINK** via public protest or in-person interactions, as long as you stay in accordance with local regulations.
- **FILE A CRIMINAL COMPLAINT** if the above actions don't go anywhere.
- If law enforcement won't help you, **SEEK A CRIMINAL WARRANT** without police aid by researching your state's code on theft by deception and conversion. If your situation meets any of the tenets of the code, you can file a request for a warrant directly with the magistrate court of the county where the crime took place.
- **FILE A CIVIL COMPLAINT** if you have no other way of getting your money back. This can be a difficult road, so consult an attorney before filing to have them determine if you have a case.
- **FILE AN OFFICIAL REPORT** to warn other consumers should all else fail.

CHAPTER 8

TrustDALE AND
BUILDING A COMMUNITY OF TRUST

DALE'S CASE STUDY FILES
A Flip That Flopped: Gaila

Gaila's dream of moving into a spacious, updated five-bedroom home quickly turned into a nightmare. One week after moving in, her septic tank backed up into her kitchen and bathroom. In addition, the technician who came to deal with the sewage backup found mold throughout the basement and on the walls. The smell from both the mold and the sewage was horrible. Gaila's new house was unlivable.

Gaila called TrustDALE for advice. Even though neither Gaila nor the company that built the house were known to us prior to her call, we decided to get to the bottom of this dire situation and see if the former owner of the house would make things right.

The former owner's name is Erick Louisius. His company name is the Pierre Louisius Group, LLC, which claims to be a leader in residential and commercial real estate development and investment.

We were not impressed with this example of his work: a flip that had flopped due to cutting corners and ignoring building codes.

It turned out the original home had been a three-bedroom "rathole," according to Louisius' description. He tried to wiggle out of the fact that the septic system was too small for the home, pointing out that it really only had three bedrooms and the bedrooms in the basement shouldn't be considered bedrooms, despite the fact that the house had been sold as a five-bedroom home.

When we gave Louisius a chance to remediate the problems with the house, it was as if we spoke different languages. He felt no remorse for his unethical behavior and had no problem with us uncovering his company's deceptive practices. He felt it would bring him more business when people saw how he turned a house-wreck into a beautiful home. The problem, of course, for any principled builder, is that his upgrade was totally cosmetic—painting over mold, for instance—and the house was still a "rathole" without spending major money to clean it up.

Since there was nothing he would do for Gaila and her family, TrustDALE brought out companies we knew provided superior service: Septic Blue to clean out the septic system and Mold Stoppers to remediate the mold issue, which was a huge job. Mold Stoppers donated their services to renew Gaila's faith in her community, and TrustDALE took care of the septic tab.

In retrospect, a home inspector indicated he hadn't inspected the septic system, though it was buried in his report. It also appears Gaila's real estate agent was in cahoots with the seller. It was incumbent on the agent to reveal that the home was a three-bedroom, not a five-bedroom. The code violation was also revealed in the inspection, which Gaila hadn't read carefully. More mindful of her reputation than Louisius was of his, the agent agreed to pay a percentage of the home's property tax for the first year.

Both the builder and the real estate agent conspired to make money off of a consumer's trusting nature. This is why it is so important to know everything you can about the character and reputation of the people you trust. "Caveat emptor" applies to houses as well as store purchases. Gaila is a smarter consumer now and will not easily be duped into a lose-win situation again.

When I started TrustDALE in 2009, I had no product or website, but I knew what I wanted to do: build a community of trust, where consumers can buy great products and services at fair prices, and companies can sell great products and services for a fair profit. After reporting on how things can go wrong for so many years, I knew how I wanted my business to guarantee things would go right. Creating a community of trust that could ensure this guarantee would require a harmony between the consumer's responsibilities and those expected of the company. Both work together to hold themselves accountable and provide the environment needed to keep TrustDALE effective and reliable.

THE ROLE OF THE CONSUMER

I believe there are three kinds of consumers. The first are those driven by fear. They stubbornly hold on to the idea they are going to get what they need for less than the asking price because they want to "get a deal." If they don't feel like they're saving money on a purchase or financial interaction, they feel taken advantage of.

The fallacy here is that price determines the value of a product or service. Fear-based consumers think that if they get something at a discount or sale price, it is a good value—although other fees are probably built into the base price. Value is actually determined by the quality of the product and the ease and attentiveness of a service in making a purchase. Consider these synonyms for value: merit, usefulness, practicality, desirability, benefit, helpfulness, effectiveness, importance, significance. Nowhere does it say "something bought at the lowest price."

I'm sure these consumers would not consider themselves greedy, but they are. The meaning of "greed" is "excessive desire" for something. Using a reduced price as the determining factor of value throws off the scale of a purchase being a win-win for buyers and sellers. Yet win-lose, or lose-win, is not sustainable in our free-market economy. Either companies and businesses suffer, or the consumer suffers.

This type of consumer is an easy target for scammers, who have no conscience when it comes to committing fraud. Once a consumer's Achilles' heel has been exposed—an excessive desire for a low, low price that isn't equated with value—that person is vulnerable to scams that take advantage of FFF and the Rip-Off Range.

Other consumers are inspired by the old carrot dangling in front of a donkey to keep it walking around in circles: they are gimmick-based. Some won't shop without a coupon, discount code, or some kind of added freebie they think enhances the value of what they decide to purchase, like BOGO (buy one, get one).

There are devoted coupon shoppers who do save money. But look in your wallet, glove compartment, car console, or that special drawer where you keep coupons. How many of them have you actually used? This is often more of a deal for the business than the consumer. It brings people in the door. And it encourages frivolous spending.

Using a gimmick is not the same as outright fraud, but it is a practice intended to distract and mislead consumers.

Using a gimmick is not the same as outright fraud, but it is a practice intended to distract and mislead consumers.

The third type of consumer is the one I hope you will be: a savvy consumer. This consumer wants a well-trained staff that can answer all questions, a product that does what it's supposed to do and that holds up over time. This consumer wants to do business with a company that is properly licensed, has liability insurance, that only hires employees who pass a background check, and that makes good on promises and guarantees. This consumer is value-driven, looking for the best opportunity for a trustworthy relationship. Instead of spending hours looking for coupons, this consumer has thought about the kind of product or service they need. This consumer researches a company's references and reviews. This consumer checks to see if a business or individual has been sued or has filed bankruptcy before signing a contract—and reads the contract before signing.

THE ROLE OF THE COMPANY

In the beginning, after preliminary research, I interviewed the owners/managers of a number of companies to find out if they were value driven, oriented toward building a trusting relationship with the consumer. I built a basic website that featured ten companies that met my standards for referrals and agreed to my Make It Right Guarantee for me to settle consumer conflicts and issues. Charging each company $1,000 a month, I went to the number-one radio station and bought $10,000 worth of advertising.

There were not a lot of visits to the website in the early days, but I started getting calls from business owners who wanted to participate in my TrustDALE partnership. Many were fed up with competing against fly-by-night businesses that fed consumers hoaxes, yet were able to pull clients away from those offering true value. Rather than running away from a service that would investigate them, business owners were welcoming the opportunity to be vetted and certified.

Nor did they retreat from the best guarantee in the marketplace: TrustDALE's $10,000 Make It Right (MIR) Guarantee, which I will describe once more because it is crucial to your trust: If the customer is dissatisfied with a product, repair, or service after first working with the company's customer service department, he/she has the right to take the grievance to TrustDALE within ninety days of the original date of purchase as reflected in a written agreement. If, after reviewing the complaint, TrustDALE agrees the customer's position is justified, the company is contractually obligated to Make It Right. The vendor must repair or replace the product or reimburse the customer for the cost of the product. Our commitment and confidence is such that if our certified business partner refuses to follow the provisions of the MIR Guarantee, TrustDALE will reimburse the consumer an amount equal to the value of the loss, up to $10,000.

The single most powerful statement any company can make is to stand behind their product or service with a guarantee to make things right if something goes wrong. My system is incredibly efficient and heads off the bad reviews and complaints on Yelp and other social media that can sink a business without giving the service provider a chance to settle things face to face.

WHERE TrustDALE FITS IN

If you look at any contract that involves mediation and arbitration, the person in charge of that is usually a person associated with the industry who is essentially paid by industry members. Even though I was being paid to publicize the businesses in the TrustDALE community, I had a reputation as a consumer investigator, seen on TV for years, who could not be influenced by power or money. I could be a third-party mediator or arbitrator to solve conflicts, not representing the company or the consumer, but focusing on the problem and a solution for both.

I think the reason businesses took to this idea was that the individuals who led companies dedicated to offering the best product or service at a fair price wanted to keep their customers happy and loyal, and not lose them due to some melodrama over a miscommunication or incident that could be negotiated. Also, TrustDALE took responsibility for the final agreement and the stress of negotiation off the shoulders of company personnel. If they signed with me, they trusted me to do the sometimes unpleasant work of mediating complaints and deciding what and how to compensate consumers in everyone's best interest.

This is TrustDALE's vision statement:

At TrustDALE, we believe in building a community of trust, where consumers get great products at fair prices, and companies sell great products for fair profit. We support our community by investigating companies to see if they meet our transparent seven-point standard. We then certify a select number of top performers, and back their performance with the best guarantee on the planet. We're not interested in adding dozens of mediocre companies just to build short-term profit—that wouldn't be honest. We believe life is better lived doing business with people we can trust. If this is the kind of community in which you'd like to live, work, and raise your family, we invite you to TrustDALE.

It's okay if you think that's corny. But if you like our vision statement, you probably identify with, and better yet live by, the tenets we espouse. Congratulations—you already belong to our TrustDALE community!

As an investigative reporter, I had the advantage of observing business practices in hundreds of fields for twenty-five years. I saw the tactics employed by fraudsters and gimmick-driven hustlers. I knew companies and individuals that operated in those zones would never agree to put a truly independent third party in charge of conflict resolution.

Out of the gate, I knew how to eliminate the fraudsters. These are the people who operate without business licenses or insurance, and who are difficult to find after a deal goes sour. Gimmick-driven companies are more difficult to authenticate. In fact, many of these companies can meet TrustDALE's seven-point standard, as described on our website, but here's the dividing line: when our team is discussing a relationship with a potential TrustDALE vendor, we describe the TrustDALE Make It Right Guarantee, and ask them—point blank—if they will not only honor it, but embrace it.

Two things can happen. They can either embrace our ideals, and adapt them into their own mission statement, or they can resist the concept entirely. Sadly, more often the alpha males who started the company or inherited the company will say, "I get what you're doing here, and I get how you could probably send me leads, *but* . . . my daddy started this company! There's no way I'm going to put YOU or anyone else in charge of customer service!" They say this with great passion, and I'm glad they do. Why? Because that's my signal that I should not recommend this company and place this company on TrustDALE. This alpha male (and sometime female) lacks the humility to accept the fact they could be in the wrong. This is the exact kind of company that will destroy itself over a social media complaint that goes viral. Here's an example.

I received a call from Tom and Debbie. They were in shock because they'd just lost $20,000 worth of heirloom jewelry and their mover wouldn't take responsibility. They acknowledged their mistake. Like most of us, they hadn't been completely prepared for their move. On move day, they had placed a handful of valuables into a locked master bathroom. They told the moving crew foreman to please leave that room untouched, and they planned to return to the house after the move to retrieve their valuables.

That wasn't the smartest move, but admit it, we've all made bone-headed mistakes.

When the couple returned to their previous residence, they found the door ajar and their precious belongings gone. They immediately called the moving company. "We were careful not to incite the owner, but simply shared that there was no other explanation than someone on their crew broke into the room and took our property," Tom explained. He said that, to his total shock, the moving company owner not only denied responsibility, but claimed his "background-checked" employees would never have stolen from his customers. The owner added insult to injury by suggesting the couple had likely "misplaced" their belongings and they should consider looking for them in other places.

The couple called both the local police and TrustDALE. We discovered through the police investigation that one of the four men on the moving crew was named John Willie Jones. Our background check found Jones was a convicted violent felon. In fact, Jones had been in and out of the state pen for most of the past twenty years, serving time for aggravated assault, battery, and possession of cocaine with the intent to distribute. How could the mover have missed this in its background check?

To this question, the owner was incredibly arrogant. When I confronted him, he responded—and I kid you not—"I background-check. I didn't say I background-decline." Wow! Claiming to "background-*check*" doesn't mean anything if the company doesn't background "decline." Remember the advice from chapter 6 under Lawsuits? This is a real-life example where knowing who's in your home really mattered. When I pressed this owner, he admitted he could hire personnel at a much lower hourly rate if they had "issues." He called them "the working poor," and actually admitted that was how he could underbid his competition. The problem was, and is, potential customers don't differentiate between "background-checked" and "background-declined." Companies that do not background-decline will send a violent convicted felon to your home. That's not right.

Everything I have described prior to this chapter relates to 1) how to identify a scam and 2) how to use my seven-step FFF/DEAL formula to avoid being scammed and instead choose a quality company. I wanted to provide consumers with a formula that's easy to remember and to enlighten them about how to be a smart consumer. The bad guys are never going away, and they are always a step ahead. But if you implement the steps of FFF and DEAL, you can trip them.

Now that you've read this book, or at least skimmed it as a reference guide, you're not alone. You can create your own community of trust by sharing what you've learned with friends and family.

You can practice this with a "trust partner," learning and using the steps of FFF and DEAL together, and calling or texting each other when you're in a tough spot and find yourself tipping into greed mode. Make it a point to share your work orders or contracts with your trust partner, whether it is your spouse or a friend. And for sure, encourage elderly consumers to have a trust partner they check with before committing over $100. In fact, volunteer to be that trust partner.

I invite you, as well, to join the TrustDALE community of trust.

Wherever you live, ask the company or vendor you are considering if they would agree, in writing, to the TrustDALE Make It Right Guarantee. We will investigate their qualifications, as we do not take on companies that don't meet our criteria. But if they do, your agreement, contract, or deal will be much more secure with TrustDALE oversight. Visit www.trustdale.com/about-us/our-guarantee to send the company an opportunity to agree.

You can also let us know how, when, and by whom you have been scammed after reading this book. We cannot take on every case, nor can we provide legal advice. But we would like to know how consumers are faring, and especially how my FFF/DEAL formula has worked for you.

I believe prevention is the best strategy for dealing with scammers and con artists, who will always be trying their best to get something for nothing.

Don't get scammed, get smart!

TrustDALE AND
BUILDING A COMMUNITY OF TRUST

- **KNOW THE THREE KINDS OF CONSUMERS**—fear-based, gimmick-driven, and savvy—and understand how their motives impact their relationship with a business.
- **UNDERSTAND HOW COMPANIES CAN DEMONSTRATE INTEGRITY** by adhering to TrustDALE's vision statement and MIR Guarantee.
- **GET A TRUST PARTNER** to hold you accountable in purchasing quality products and/or services.
- **JOIN TrustDALE'S COMMUNITY OF TRUST** and share your experiences to empower others in finding a balance between fair price and fair profit.
- **CONTACT TrustDALE** with feedback on how the FFF/DEAL formula has worked for you.

APPENDIX

COMMON SCAMS, CONS, AND SCHEMES

ADVANCE-FEE SCHEMES

Paying for services, products, or assistance in advance is always risky. If you don't know the individual or business entity you are dealing with, you have no way of knowing their motives. This is why you must research the legitimacy of anyone who wants money up front, and secure proof that what you have paid for will be delivered in a timely manner. As Tanqunika's online car broker story shows, it can be very hard to track down someone who has already been paid, and then convince them to deliver the goods you were promised.

Advice: NEVER give money up front to a person you've never met and haven't checked out.

FRAUD AGAINST SENIORS

This is a broad category, limited only by the imagination and creativity of the fraudsters. The primary delivery mechanism is by telephone, but the internet is quickly gaining. Most of the ingredients inherent in all the scams listed here are present in elder scams. The difference is the perpetrator is intentionally targeting older people. Seniors are especially vulnerable when it comes to threats to their security, health, or children. Few events are more painful than learning your mom or dad has been taken advantage of and they were too embarrassed to ask you for advice or tell you after the fact. It is my goal to arm seniors and their younger loved ones with the ability to perceive the elements of a scam—not just the scam itself.

Advice: Be your parent's trust partner. If you can't do it personally, find someone who can.

IDENTITY THEFT

The great Equifax security breach of 2018 was one of the largest cases of identity theft in the twenty-first century. Computers have changed all our lives, and the way we do business. But living in the "Age of Information" also means our personal data, and all of our financial data, is at risk of being stolen and misused. The Equifax cybersecurity incident involved thousands of passports and driver's licenses, as well as the Social Security numbers of nearly all of the 146 million affected consumers. The name, address, phone number, and birthdate of at least one person in every family in America were leaked.

But someone is attempting to steal your identity pretty much every day of the year. You can be bombarded by phone calls and emails from entities posing as your bank, the IRS, stores you shop at, and your internet provider asking you to update your personal information. Robocalls are programed to contact you round the clock. Never respond to these solicitations. Instead, make direct contact with the businesses represented and check in with and alert them if you are concerned.

Other scammers are much more patient. You might get a solicitation from your gas company and all they need is the last four digits of your social. What's the harm in that? One week later, a person who claims to be with your pharmacy calls to get the three middle digits of your social. Finally, the most innocent contact asks for the state where you were born. What you don't realize is you've just surrendered your full social security number to three people working toward the same goal. You see, the first three digits of your social are based on your birth state, so they have your number without even asking!

Advice: Create a fake identity when filling forms that ask for your personal information but are not entitled to require it by law. Freeze your credit with each credit bureau and ask each for a free credit report once per year.

INTERNET AUCTION FRAUD

The internet has all sorts of ways to keep track of what you like and may want to buy. The ads that continuously pop up reflect your online habits. If you click on an item listed in an internet marketplace, the seller will want payment in advance, of course. Millions of consumer dollars are lost every year to internet fraud because the item arrives and it's not what you thought you were buying, or you wire the money and the item never arrives.

Advice: Never wire money to an unknown source or use a debit card that takes money directly from your bank account. Use a credit card so you have the option of disputing the charge if the item doesn't show up.

MORTGAGE SCAMS

The challenge with this scam is that authentic reverse-mortgage opportunities do exist, so consumers must learn to recognize the difference. Legitimate reverse-mortgage plans provide income for seniors who own or have significant equity in their homes. They receive immediate cash and don't have to repay the money until they no longer can afford the mortgage, the home is sold, or they die.

The red flag occurs when the financial organization offers the senior a complicated package that includes contracts for home improvements, or the senior learns the mortgage application has fallen through at the last minute and an unaffordable traditional mortgage is offered as part of a high-pressure sale. The truth is that reverse-mortgage scams exist in more forms than this book has room to describe, thus you'll understand my desire to teach you to recognize the common denominators of all scams.

Advice: In the event you or someone you love is offered a reverse mortgage, make certain it is insured by the FHA (Federal Housing Administration). Get proof of that insurance from the FHA, not the person selling the mortgage. Finally, never sign any documents you don't fully understand.

ONLINE VEHICLE SALE SCAMS

You read about what happened to Tanqunika when she bought a car online. There are many ways of marketing this scam: a seller might share a story of medical hardship as the reason they are selling a fantastic car so cheaply, or maybe they have to move out of the country quickly to relocate for a new job. The point will be that there's a valid reason for pricing the car so low and wanting the cash immediately. A seller might even set up a phone call with a third party who will back up the offer's credibility.

There are so many ways this deal can go bad that I would never recommend purchasing a car from an unknown corporate or private seller over the internet.

Advice: If the person wants you to wire the payment or use codes from pre-paid gift cards, you know for sure this is a setup to take your money.

PONZI SCHEMES

This fraud is always presented as an investment opportunity. Your return is often guaranteed, or if there is risk, you might already have great confidence and trust in the person making the offer. Ponzi schemes are different than most scams in that there is often an early impressive return on your investment. I busted a financial planner once who had gained the confidence of an elderly couple and became their money manager. He created false financial documents for the first six consecutive months that showed impressive returns on their portfolio. He then convinced them to invest their entire life savings into, I'm not kidding, a castle in Ireland that was being converted to condominiums. A year and a half later, the couple discovered there was no castle and their retirement savings were gone.

How did this con man gain their confidence so easily? He was a deacon in their church.

People new to the world of Ponzi schemes associate it with Bernard (Bernie) Madoff, the Palm Beach financial advisor who swindled approximately five thousand clients out of almost $65 billion. He was sentenced to 150 years in prison and ordered to repay $170 billion in 2009. But it is Charles (Carlo) Ponzi, the man for whom the scheme was named, who swindled Americans out of $20 million in the 1920s.

Advice: Remember the two ingredients that are often present in similar schemes: the perpetrator claims to have a sophisticated level of knowledge in the subject matter, and his story is so convincing, you don't take the time or effort to verify his credibility with an independent third party. Very often, he or she weaves in a theme of "let's keep this between us," because if everyone knew they would either want in too, or put a stop to it.

But there's always an automatic stop to it—when your money is gone and your trusted financial advisor has disappeared to live a discreet but high-end lifestyle in a foreign country (if they're not caught).

PRIZE SCAMS

When I was working with Clark Howard, author of books and guides, and host of Clark.com and multiple podcasts, all focusing on saving money, we investigated a prize scam in Atlanta and in Phoenix. Letters were sent through the mail announcing the recipient had won money. However, a processing fee was needed in order to send the money. In one scam it was $72.59, in another it was $10.

Common to both scams was that neither of the con artists listed real business names, and both used PO boxes instead of street addresses, making it harder to track down the person behind the letter. We were able to bust both cases with the aid of the US Postal Inspector's office.

Although the police said they had not been able to track down the man in the first scam, Gerald Trappier, who promised $10,000 for $72.59, we found the guy's name in the phone book and confronted him. He denied knowing anything about the letter, but when police did get involved, they noted he had about $20,000 in his bank account, which showed up in deposits of around $75. He finally admitted it was his bank account, but that he had "opened it for a friend."

The letter was much the same in the second case, in Arizona. The windfall was for up to $10,000, but the processing fee was only $10. We found out who the owner of the PO box was, and were told he picked up about nine trays of mail a day, sometimes up to 4,500 letters—all with a check for $10. The two men involved in this scam vowed to follow the rules of the postal service, but all they did was change the language of the letter. They stopped sending out the old version, and sent out five new versions.

Advice: Prize scams are often the hardest to avoid because they promise instant gratification. Giving money to a stranger to receive something you didn't earn never ends well.

PYRAMID SCHEMES

This con comes in two traditional forms. The first is an offer for you to make a payment to join a group of people who are "sharing the love" or "paying it forward." Individuals put a few thousand dollars into this "giving" program and then wait for the return on their investment, which is supplied by the people who put money down after them. This is a perfect business model for scamming people in groups that are oriented toward faith, positive thinking . . . and a need for a cash windfall.

The second type of pyramid scheme involves a product. It's called a multi-level marketing program. Some multi-level marketing programs (MLMs) are legit. Here's how to know the difference. Legal MLMs will earn money from selling a legitimate product, and the bulk of the revenue is earned through the sale. The second type of MLM, which is not legit, derives the bulk of the company's revenue not from the sale of the product, but rather recruitment. A friend, or stranger, tells you about something that is "unique," "amazing," or just plain cheaper than usual that they have started selling, which is a fun sideline. They offer to let you join their "network" for some kind of membership fee so you, too, can get in on the fun and profit. You don't immediately realize your friend's profit comes from recruiting people to work under her to sell the product, which is negligible.

Advice: Ask your friend point-blank which makes them more money, recruiting or selling the product. If they have a hard time giving you an answer, that's your red flag. Get out!

THE NIGERIAN PRINCE LETTER

If you receive a phone call or message from someone claiming they will share amazing riches with you if only you can help them with money up front, hang up or delete it immediately. They may also claim to be some sort of official in Nigeria who tells you a story about a civil war or coup that has changed the governing authority, resulting in this person having to deposit his oil money in a bank the authorities don't know about. You will be asked to wire a small processing fee, and told you will get that back and more for your trouble. The kicker here is you may actually receive the promised check, written for, say, $10,000. You rush to the bank to deposit the check, perhaps even before you've wired the fee. Here's what the scammer knows that you probably don't: it will take the bank three business days to find out the check is fake or there are insufficient funds in the account from where it is drawn.

I know these two examples seem too obvious to fall for, but it happens hundreds, perhaps thousands, of times every single day! You see it as an individual ruse; con artists see it as a numbers game. They cast their net for literally millions of fish, knowing they'll catch just a few thousand. This process is made even easier through the advent of robocalling. The scam is nearly impossible to police because the letters, emails, and calls are coming from overseas.

Advice: No one is going to give you free money. Resist the urge to click on the ad, and definitely don't respond.

TELEMARKETING SCAMS

At this writing, American consumers are being inundated with robocalls. If you live under a rock and aren't familiar with auto-mated computer calling, thousands of numbers can be dialed at one time, and around the clock. An automated message is acti-vated when a caller answers. Often the area code is the same as yours, or the number is similar to one you might think belongs to a friend. Americans received more than twenty-six billion such calls in 2018, and if Congress doesn't act, experts expect that number to triple in 2019 and beyond.

There is a federal Do Not Call Registry. But scammers, especially if they are foreign-based, don't respect it because the sheer scale of the problem means they can't be held accountable. In fact, a technique called "spoofing" allows our American phone systems to create a false identity for the origin of the call. It could be a trusted local pharmacy. Yet when you answer, it is a company claiming you once sought them out to purchase an extended warranty for your car.

Chances are, these scammers got your number by purchasing your personal information, including information about your car, from legitimate entities, but that's where the legitimacy stops. These crooks are experts at keeping you on the line, convincing you the warranty is not only a great deal but in your best interest, and can hook you before you know it.

What if you get a call at 4:00 a.m. and it sounds like your hysterical sobbing son or daughter, who hands the phone to a man who claims to be her attorney? There's been a horrendous car accident and your child is allegedly at fault for the death of a second driver. The attorney claims there is a swiftly closing window in which a $4,000 bond can be paid to keep your loved one out of jail over the weekend and allow time to make a plan. The attorney advises you to go to the nearest 24/7 drugstore, where you can purchase gift cards or prepaid debit cards from which you can read the code on the back over the phone so the attorney and bonding authorities can receive payment.

Sound ridiculously farfetched? IT HAPPENS EVERY DAY! People in emotion-driven crises act illogically. In one true story, the father didn't realize he'd been duped until after he'd returned home, when his wife asked him what his daughter had actually said. It turned out he hadn't understood her at all through the crying. That's the moment he and his wife realized it was possibly a scam. The sting of their $4,000 loss was slightly reduced by the sound of their daughter's voice calling them back when she awoke and noticed they'd left a panicked message asking her to call as soon as possible.

Folks, these con artists mean business! They're evil, and they are good at what they do.

Advice: Don't answer your phone if you don't recognize the number. If it's important, the caller will leave a message.

Likewise, don't automatically believe the story you hear from the person on the other end of the call. Scammers often pretend to be law enforcement or court officials to increase temporary credibility. If you can't get a street address or some other contact information to verify legitimacy, hang up!

To see the FBI's complete list of the most common scams, visit https://www.fbi.gov/scams-and-safety/common-fraud-schemes.

ACKNOWLEDGMENTS

I would like to thank my wife, Angie, for her patience, loyalty, and faith, as well as my children, Adam and Jessica, for being who they are. I would also like to thank my business mentor Billy Corey, not only for helping to create TrustDALE, but for his steadfast support to see it succeed. Thank you, Mike Stresser, Denton Harris, and Ray Fisher for your endless patience and savvy advice. Thank you, Clark Howard, for teaching me how to put empathy into action. My brother, Bruce Cardwell, has been with me from the start, and we wouldn't be where we are without his devotion and talent. My close friend and attorney Tom Clyde is the best copy editor I've ever met. TrustDALE's general manager, Laura Lovejoy, has been invaluable, along with the dedication of the entire TrustDALE team, which spends every day working to safeguard consumers. My co-author Judy Kirkwood's insights and writing skills turned my consumer-investigation experience and ideas into a handbook I hope you will enjoy and use.

Last but not least, I am grateful for the consumers who have shared with me their stories of disappointment and frustration at being scammed. It's not easy to admit you lost money to a con artist, and I am truly humbled by your faith in me and in TrustDALE. I am also gratified by TrustDALE's partners, who are dedicated to providing the best service at fair prices, as well as to upholding TrustDALE's Make It Right Guarantee for 100 percent customer satisfaction. AAMCO and Havoline Xpress Lube in particular have been very generous in restoring consumers' trust in the marketplace by providing their services in times of need.

ABOUT THE AUTHOR

Consumer Investigator Dale Cardwell is a six-time Emmy Award–winning journalist, author, speaker, television, and podcast host. Throughout his thirty-five-year career, Dale has busted bad guys, protected consumers, and saved taxpayers millions. In 2009 he launched his consumer research and referral website TrustDALE.com, where consumers can find certified companies that have met a transparent seven-point investigative standard.

Now that you've read *Don't Get Scammed: Get Smart!*, we hope that you have all the tools you need to send scammers packing, and not with your hard-earned money! However, the journey does not stop here. Visit TrustDALE.com to find reputable companies in your area that have passed Dale Cardwell's seven-point inspection, and receive quality services from businesses you can trust.

We want to hear from you!

Have you been burned in the past by a shady business OR would you like to rave about a company that gave you a five-star experience? Please let us know by visiting trustdale.com/contact. You might even end up featured on one of our social media pages below.

Follow TrustDALE online to hear stories from consumers just like you and to continue getting valuable and timely tips from Dale.

@TrustDale

@trustdale

TrustDALE TV